45 Master Characters

Mythic Models for Creating Original Characters

Victoria Schmidt

WRITER'S DIGEST BOOKS
Cincinnati, Ohio
http://www.writersdigest.com

Movie stills reprinted with permission of PhotoFest, Inc., New York. Black and white line art from Dover Pictoral Archive Series: *Women: A Pictoral Archive from Ninteenth-Century Sources*; *Beardsley's Illustrations for Le Morte Darthur, Men: A Pictoral Archive from Ninteenth-Century Sources*; and *Weapons & Armor: A Pictoral Archive of Woodcuts & Engravings*.

Visit our Web site at www.writersdigest.com for information on more resources for writers.

To receive a free weekly e-mail newsletter delivering tips and updates about writing and about Writer's Digest products, register directly at our Web site http://newsletters .fwpublications.com.

11   10   09   5   4   3

Library of Congress has cataloged hardcover edition as follows:

Schmidt, Victoria.
    45 Master Characters: Mythic models for creating original characters / by Victoria Schmidt.
        p.   cm.
    Includes index.
    ISBN-13: 978-1-58297-069-1 (hc: alk. paper)
    ISBN-10: 1-58297-069-6 (hc: alk. paper)
    ISBN-13: 978-1-58297-522-1 (pbk.: alk. paper)
    ISBN-10: 1-58297-522-1 (pbk.: alk. paper)
        1. Characters and characteristics in literature. 2. Fiction—Technique. I. Title.

PN218.S36   2001
808.3'97—dc21   2001026288
                                                            CIP

Edited by Meg Leder
Designed by Angela Wilcox
Cover design and photo collage by Jeffrey Martin
Production coordinated by Mark Griffin

fw
F•W PUBLICATIONS, INC.

This book is dedicated:

To my family—Stephen, Sandra, Angela, Kimberly and Barbara—

thanks for sharing your archetypes with me and for all your

encouragement.

And most of all to Thomas Fressle—I am ever grateful.

ABOUT THE AUTHOR

 Victoria began her career as a screenwriter for film and television. She is a graduate of the film program at UCLA and also holds a master's degree in screenwriting from Loyola Mary-mount University.

She has written several original screenplays, two television series and is currently writing a novel. She lives in Los Angeles where she occasionally works as a story consultant. See her website at: http://www.CharactersJourney.com.

TABLE OF CONTENTS

Introduction

I wrote this book for every writer who has ever felt weighed down by the rules of fiction writing. The theories and information presented here are meant to offer writers a way out of the stifling maze of structure, form and rules surrounding fiction writing. It is a book that honors the spark of passion and vision within the heart of every writer.

When you, the writer, sit down to tell your story, you are often energized and enthusiastic about your idea. A flash of inspiration has drawn you to the blank page as you eagerly pour out what you feel in your heart is a great story.

Then somewhere along the way you start questioning whether your story is really a good story after all. Will anyone want to read it? You can't figure out where your story is going, and you wind up comparing it to other stories on the bestseller lists. Soon, in the midst of outlines and character changes, you give up and move on to another idea, only to repeat the pattern. What has happened? You've gotten so bogged down with structure and plotting, you lost the creative spark that made you face that blank page in the first place.

I'm presenting these archetypes to show you the unique characters that are available to work with. Once you've gotten the basic idea of archetypes down, you can do whatever you wish with them. They are truly the foundation your characters will stand upon. They'll add life and energy to your stories.

I also present the feminine and masculine journeys your characters may explore. These journeys can help preserve the spark you had when you began writing. With nine plot stages, you can easily map out the direction of your story. You can sit down and write and write and write without worrying about where your story is going.

How does this preserve creativity? Aren't the archetypes simply overused stereotypes? Don't the nine stages become rules themselves? No to both. The archetypes preserve your creative spark by giving you a blueprint to work from. They help you to delve deeper into your character by answering "What makes this character tick?" They push you to think about the character's history and circumstance, and they stimulate you into developing scenes that are rich with archetypal quirks and idiosyncrasies. The nine stages merely show a direction, a progression of events that map out a story line and help develop a character arc. There can be as many as a hundred or as few as five pages in between each stage. It's totally up to you.

My Journey to Write This Book

What sparked this book in me? It started when I was at film school and I was told that I couldn't write a script about a female hero because those stories don't sell. (As I write this I see Julia Roberts is the highest-paid actor among men and women. Go figure.) Needless to say I was very upset. What I had to say didn't matter? It wasn't commercial enough?

In *The Bridge to Wholeness: A Feminine Alternative to the Hero Myth* by Jean Benedict Raffa, I read a quote by Joseph Campbell: "There are no models in our mythology for an individual woman's quest. Nor is there any model for the male in marriage to an individuated female."

So I spent the next few years searching for the female hero's journey so I could prove everyone wrong. Typical bright-eyed writer! One day I was watching *The Wizard of Oz*, and I realized it was close to what women go through. Was this the only example women had? I took every class imaginable on the subject, and I learned a great deal about myths, writing and feminist theory. Still, no one had any answers for me.

A few months later, as I was going through a "dark night of the soul" experience, my own personal descent, I found a book about the descent of the goddess Inanna. Everything fell into place. Here I had found the oldest myth in history (dated 2000 B.C.), and not only was a huge part of it about a female hero but it was also about the female journey into the self. I was living this journey on a personal level, and I knew it inside and out. Once I saw how *The Wizard of Oz* fit the model I knew I had found the female myth. Much later, when I went to see the film *Titanic*, I instantly knew why the film did so well. It wasn't just that Leonardo DiCaprio was cute and young girls liked him. It was that this film unknowingly mapped out the feminine journey and young girls unconsciously resonated with it. This was the female *Star Wars*.

Jack Heffron at Writer's Digest Books immediately loved this book idea and asked me, "Well, what about the male hero?" I thought, *that's already been done to death*, but I explored it anyway. It was then that I realized the male journey wasn't as clear-cut as I originally thought. The male hero was just learning to descend on his inner journey, and it would take him much later to do it, whereas the female hero would descend much sooner.

As I looked closer, I also found that women were not the only ones going on the female journey but that a few men were going on the descent as well. (I will later show how the film *American Beauty* is an example of this.) I realized archetypal journals were beyond gender—that the journeys I had found were a part of both men and women, and were more appropriately titled feminine and masculine journeys so they could include both sexes.

The archetypes part of this book was sparked by a need for more well-developed female characters. Often it seems as if roles for female heroes could have just as easily been written for a male hero. These roles lack the nuances of the female experiences. They act like men and don't ring true.

When they do ring true, it is often only as the Seductive Muse or the Nurturer type, and as the archetypes show, there are many other types to portray. As I worked on the male archetype section, I realized the range of male characters also; consider both the Recluse and the Artist. Using the archetypes to fully develop your characters can make your story stand out.

So that's my journey with this book. My hope is that this book inspires your writing and adds fuel to that first spark that contains your amazing story idea. May you be blessed with many days of enthusiastic writing.

I **Getting Started**

Chapter 1

What Are Archetypes, and Why Should Writers Use Them?

"Archetype: Image, ideal, or pattern that has come to be considered a universal model. Archetypes are found in mythology, literature, and the arts, and are . . . largely unconscious image patterns that cross cultural boundaries."

—Encarta

Why should you use archetypes when designing a story? In my experience almost every writer comes face-to-face with what I call the "page thirty blahs." You're writing your novel or screenplay. You have a wonderful idea. You spend days outlining and writing the first thirty pages. Then suddenly something happens. You lose steam. The pages get harder and harder to write. The momentum you had going slows down. Writer's block looms in the distance, and you lose excitement in the masterpiece you're writing.

You think to yourself, "Maybe the premise wasn't that good after all? Maybe I should work on a different story? This one just won't move."

Don't give up on your story. The good news is that most of the time the problem isn't with your story but with your characters. How can your story move forward if your driving force—character—is running on empty? If you think of your character in terms of the librarian stereotype, you only get a general idea of the character. It doesn't tell you anything about her motivations, goals or fears. How can you make new, exciting discoveries about your character if she's nothing but a stereotype or a blank page in your mind? You may have plot points, but did you think about how your character will react to the situations those plot points put her in? This reaction drives the story forward, not the plot points. A character doesn't decide to go into a burning building because that's what your plot point says he should do—he goes inside because it's in his nature to do so.

Have you heard the story of "The Scorpion and the Frog"? A frog comes upon a scorpion and pleads for his life. The scorpion says he will not kill the frog if the frog takes him across the river. The frog asks, "How do I know you won't kill me as I carry you?" The scorpion replies, "If I were to strike you we would both surely die." Thinking it over the frog agrees and halfway across the river the scorpion strikes the frog in the back. As they both start to drown the frog asks, "Why did you strike me? Now we will both die." The scorpion replies with his last breath, "Because it is in my nature." What is in the nature of your character? Using archetypes can help you discover the answer to this question.

Luke Skywalker—Dorothy—Xena—Captain Ahab

When you think of these characters almost immediately a very real sense of who they are jumps out at you. They are not bland one-dimensional characters but real people we can relate to. They invoke strong emotion in us; we want to be just like them or we want to be completely opposite. The stories they inhabit are not what make them memorable; what makes them memorable is the depth of their character, their three-dimensionality. Not every character has to be noble and perfect; Xena's dark side makes her complex, human and interesting.

All of these characters embody a universal archetype, which helps them to inhabit a strong character arc. A character arc shows the changes a character goes through during a story. Every great protagonist learns and grows from her experiences within a story. Your character needs to emerge at the end of your story as a new person who has learned something from her journey.

The master archetypes discussed in this book are grouped into thirteen male and female supporting characters and thirty-two male and female heroes and villains. In addition, you'll find information on the archetypal patterns for thirteen supporting characters.

Luke Skywalker (Mark Hamill) in *Star Wars* can be seen in the Male Messiah archetype while Captain Ahab from *Moby Dick* is seen in the King. Dorothy (Judy Garland) in *The Wizard of Oz* definitely embodies the Maiden archetype, while Xena (Lucy Lawless) in *Xena: Warrior Princess* fits the Amazon perfectly. Although these characters are much more than their archetypes, archetypes inspire the discoveries and details that make them interesting.

What Are Archetypes?

To a psychologist, archetypes are mental fingerprints revealing the details of a patient's personality. To a writer, archetypes are the blueprints for building well-defined characters be they heroes, villains or supporting characters.

In Jungian psychology there are seven master archetypes as seen in the Greek goddesses and gods. This book looks at these archetypes from the perspective of the writer and adds one additional archetype of the Messiah, the powerful enlightened being who is not explored in Jungian thought. As movies like *The Matrix* become popular, I believe we will see a lot of this archetype in future stories and films.

Archetypes are an invaluable tool often overlooked by writers. By their very nature they force you to delve deeper into your characters, to see them as not just "Character 1" or "Librarian" but as a type of person who responds in very specific ways to the conflict within your story. All too often writers create several characters who act exactly like the writer himself; archetypes help you to avoid this.

In using archetypes, the essence of your character is narrowed down so she jumps off the page at the reader instead of blending in with all the other characters. Each archetype has her own set of motivations, fears and cares that move her as well as the plot forward.

Once an archetype blueprint is selected, family, culture, class and age shape how the character expresses that essence. It's important to know every aspect of the character in detail in order to make decisions about what she would do in any given situation the plot throws her in.

Archetypes vs. Stereotypes

Beware of books that present stereotypes as archetypes, which is exactly the opposite of what a writer should use to create exciting new characters. Stereotypes are oversimplified generalizations about people usually stemming from one person's prejudice. Archetypes aren't formed from one individual's view of people but from the entire human race's experience of people. Judgment and assumptions are absent.

Describing a character as a "typical librarian" asks you to join in the assumption that all librarians are quiet spinsters. This description limits the character's growth and range of possibilities. What are the hidden fears and secrets of this character? What motivates her? An archetype will help you answer these questions.

Stereotypes may be used to describe an archetype but a stereotype is only a shallow imitation, a small piece of the bigger picture you can use to create your characters.

Working With an Archetype
Expand Your Vision of Your Main Character

Pick a character you want to write about. If you've written a story already, then pick a character you would like to spice up in a rewrite. Before you select an archetype, figure out how you already envision this character.

Your hero stands invisible before you like a cartoon character waiting to be drawn. Close your eyes for a moment and imagine this character coming to life in front of you as you answer these questions:

○ **Face**—Is it full or narrow? Why? What can we learn about her history, age, occupation and class from her face? Are her eyes perpetually sad looking or harsh?

○ **Skin**—How dark is it? Is it the soft skin of a pampered man or the rough skin of a blue-collar man?

○ **Hair**—Is it long, short, curly or stringy?

Most mothers cut their hair short due to lack of grooming time in the mornings with a baby around, unless they can afford a nanny.

○ **Age**—What is the best age to convey the struggle of this character? If your character is a divorced mother who has given up her livelihood to raise a family then it would be much more dramatic for her to be starting over at forty years of age than at twenty. See chapters ten and twenty-four for information on a character's life stages.

○ **Body type**—Is she a full-figured woman with the hips of a mother who bore five children? Is she lean and muscular like an accomplished athlete?

⦸ **Style—**Is he trendy or twenty years behind? Does he dress too old for his age?

⦸ **Your impressions—**Do you like this character? Why? Find out why you want to spend the next year writing about this character. It will help you to persuade the reader to love him, too.

Which Archetypal Model Does This Character Embody the Most?

Now figure out the basic personality elements of this character. These questions will help you see the archetypal pattern emerge.

⦸ Is she introverted or extroverted?

⦸ Does he solve problems using instincts, logical thinking or emotion?

⦸ Does she want to change the world?

⦸ Where does he live? Describe the bedroom. It's the most private and secretive room in the house.

⦸ How does she feel about her appearance?

⦸ How does he feel about family and children?

⦸ What does she think about men and marriage?

⦸ What are his hobbies?

⦸ What type of friends does she have?

⦸ What does he consider to be fun?

⦸ How does she feel about her sexuality?

⦸ Does he need to have control of his environment?

⦸ What do other characters say about her when she leaves the room?

⦸ Does he take life seriously or act like a kid most of the time?

⦸ Where would she spend a Sunday afternoon? By herself in the bookstore? At a luncheon party with friends? Looking over files for work?

Now you have basic answers to help you see which archetype your character fits into most. As you review the archetypes in the following chapters, you'll begin to see which archetype seems "right"—it will be the archetype that matches your character's traits and will help you grow your character in new ways. Later you'll be able to see if you have character elements that don't "fit" the archetype. Consistency is what makes a character feel alive to a reader. For example, we expect a Father's Daughter to have some trouble in a room filled with children. If she were to embrace such a situation and be perfect at it, she wouldn't feel real at all.

Think of J.C. Wiatt (Diane Keaton), the Father's Daughter, in the movie *Baby Boom*. It took her a while just to figure out how to change a diaper. Also think of Detective John Kimble (Arnold Schwarzenegger), the Protector, in *Kindergarten Cop*. He has major headaches when he's with children. He treats them as if they were in military school, and it takes him a while to learn how to deal with them properly.

Chapter 2

How to Use the Archetypes

Now that your hero stands drawn before you, she needs to have her personality colored in. Along with a character sketch and insight into archetypal psychology, the following chapters provide the tools to help you answer these questions for each master archetype: What does your character *care* about? What does she *fear*? What *motivates* her? How do other characters *view* her?

What Does Your Character Care About?

In a general sense all characters care about something. Traditionally writers are asked the following questions to define a character—"If your character was stranded on a desert island what are the three things he would want to have?" or "What would he miss the most if his house burned down?" Each archetype has a different set of values that dictates what these things are. In some cases what the hero cares most about isn't a material object or person but a way of life. An Amazon woman would rather die than give up her independence, like the heroes in *Thelma & Louise* do. A King would abandon his children if they refused to obey his rules.

You want to know what this character cares about not only to tell us who she is but to create obstacles by placing the thing she cares about most in danger as she tries to reach her goal. While a character cares deeply about reaching her goal, she may care more about saving a friend's life and will let the goal slip out of her reach to save her friend. Think of Xena (the Amazon) from *Xena: Warrior Princess*. The plotline may take her to a village she has to save from an evil warlord, but suddenly Gabrielle, her trusted friend and soul mate, is kidnapped. Xena will drop everything to save her even if it means destroying the village.

Don't let archetypes dictate the plotline to you. Because a character cares deeply about getting married like the Matriarch, it doesn't mean you're a slave to writing a plot that deals with marriage if you choose this archetype. Whatever plotline you place your character in, this desire will filter into the dialogue and subtext of your scenes and chapters.

What Does Your Character Fear?

What would give her nightmares? If she heard a noise in the dead of night how would she react? What would she envision is making the noise?

The best tests a character can come up against stem from fear. It's much more suspenseful to see a character who is deathly afraid of water jump into the ocean to save a loved one than it is to see an Olympic swimmer do the same thing.

The fears a character possesses come from the psychological aspect of their archetype mixed in with their past experience. For example, the Businessman prefers city life and civilization. Combine this with a fear of wild animals due to a camping accident as a child and you have a character terrified of the outdoors. Perhaps he confines himself to his home in the city and the four walls of his office. One day his boss asks him to travel to a remote country area for an account he's working on. Since his job is what he cares most about, he is forced to face his fears.

Ask yourself what happened to this character at a young age to create this fear. You can then sprinkle this information to the reader along the way.

What Motivates Your Character?

Linda Segar's book *Making a Good Script Great* outlines the seven character motivators that "explain what drives us, what we want and what's at stake if we don't get it."

They are:

○ **Survival**—The basic need to live and survive.

○ **Safety and Security**—Once basic needs are taken care of we need to feel safe, secure and protected.

○ **Love and Belonging**—Once we have a home we desire a sense of family or community or connection. Unconditional love and acceptance.

○ **Esteem and Self-Respect**—Is earned love and respect for what you've done in your life, to be looked up to and to be recognized.

○ **The Need to Know and Understand**—The search for knowledge. We have a natural curious desire to know how things work and how things fit together.

○ **The Aesthetic**—The need for balance, a sense of order in life, a sense of being connected to something greater than ourselves. Can be spiritual.

○ **Self-Actualization**—To express ourselves; to communicate who we are; to actualize our talents, skills and abilities whether or not we are publicly recognized.

Each archetype resonates with one of these motivators in a special way. Archetypes themselves are very connected to these motivating forces—they drive characters to do the crazy things they do, as you'll see in the coming chapters.

How Do Other Characters View Your Character?

How do your character's clothes and desires fit in with her archetype? How would we recognize this archetype on the street? For example, an Amazon woman would prefer to wear comfortable clothing like sweatpants while a Businessman would choose a plainly designed suit.

What do other characters say about him behind his back? How do they read his actions and opinions? Are they afraid of him? Are they jealous of her? Do they have an accurate view of him? Will this character allow others to get to know her or does she hide her true self?

Nontraditional Uses

Be creative when using the archetypes. They are merely meant to be guides. For example, when I say the archetype known as the King—a man who loves to be in control, who's neat and organized, who leads others, gives advice, etc.—it would be easy to think of someone like Tony Soprano (James Gandolfini) from *The Sopranos* fitting in with this archetype, but Jerry Seinfeld from *Seinfeld* fits this archetype as well. Everyone comes over to his house and seeks his advice; he's always in control; he's neat and organized. His character is a comedic twist to this archetype.

Think of the Amazon archetype; Xena, Nikita (Peta Wilson) in *La Femme Nikita*, and Lieutenant Ellen L. Ripley (Sigourney Weaver) in *Alien* all fit this archetype but so does Gracie Hart (Sandra Bullock) in *Miss Congeniality*. She's an Amazon woman who's forced into entering a beauty pageant yet knows nothing about hair, makeup or style. Be creative with the archetypes.

Which Archetype Should You Choose?

If you've developed your story already, consider how different it would be with each of the different archetypes in the lead role. Pick three archetypes and write a one-page outline of your story for each type. You may be surprised at all the new twists and plot points you come up with based on an archetype's fears and desires.

Remember to pick an archetype that has room to grow the most as a result of the obstacles he faces in your story. Put a King into a story where he loses control of everyone. Put a Father's Daughter into a story that takes her into the woods and the wilderness. Archetypal characters must learn something from the experiences you give them so they become more than just their archetype.

To begin, select an archetype that interests you and see if using his fears against him would be fun and challenging. It may even be comedic.

Combining Archetypes: Is an Amazon Always an Amazon?

Essentially we may have many archetypes within our personalities but one is usually dominant. Within each archetype I ask 'What happened at an early age to cultivate this archetype in your character?' There is usually an event during the developmental years that causes us to adapt to survive, the way we adapt shows our dominate archetype.

When we are under any type of stress this dominant archetype always takes over. A Nurturer can believe in independence and equality but that doesn't make her an Amazon. Does she act to enforce these beliefs? Or are they just part of her backstory? In the major scenes is she nurturing or speaking out? Basically we can all believe in saving the rain forest but how many of us tie ourselves to a tree and fight for it like an Amazon would?

Likewise an Amazon who raises children, lets say, doesn't cower when faced by the villain at the end of the story because at heart she's still an Amazon.

✪

Once you've drawn your character outline and colored in the foundations of his personality you're ready for the final step of plotting and outlining the character arc in the journey section of this book.

Exercises

✪ If you haven't done it already, pick out three archetypes and write a one-page outline of your story for each one. Pay attention to how each archetype can change the plot or add new twists to it.

✪ Write two pages, long hand, on why your character is the archetype you have chosen. If he's The King, write something like this: He loves to have as much control as possible especially over his home life. When he goes to work he frequently yells at the young computer-savvy kids in the office who make him feel stupid and inadequate for not knowing about the latest software.

✪ Let your character talk to you. Write one page in first person letting the character tell you how she feels about the goal you're giving her.

II **Creating Female Heroes and Villains**

Chapter 3

Aphrodite

The Seductive Muse
and the Femme Fatale

From the depths of the ocean, the realm of emotions, Aphrodite emerges a perfect image of beauty. She covers herself with an implied modesty but does not crouch or hide from your gaze. She charms you with an innocent smile all the while knowing the hold she has on you. She steps from the sea, her hair flowing in the breeze. The sea creatures give up their lives just to follow her onto land and gaze at her for one moment longer. She takes in the sights and smells of her surroundings as if she's a child in a strange land. Everything is fascinating and beautiful to her. Desire and love follow her, turning wise men into fools.

The Seductive Muse

The seductive muse is a strong woman who knows what she wants. She has a lust for life, forever satisfying all her senses. The gods bestowed on her gifts of creativity, beauty, love and abundance, which make her driven to creative projects that show the world who she is. She's a great inventor and visionary who often sees the simplest solution to life's problems. She's the child who tells the trucker to let the air out of his tires when he can't figure out how to get his tall truck through the highway tunnel.

A deep longing for love and connection with one man fills her heart, but she can't give up the thrill of the chase. She needs many relationships and sensual experiences to keep her stimulated and alive. She can't do anything alone unless it's an intense creative activity that requires deep focus. A natural healer, she cares deeply about other people's feelings and tries

With her desire for the drama of high society and passionate affairs, Gustave Flaubert's Emma Bovary displays the qualities of the Seductive Muse archetype.

to help them heal their wounds.

In our culture, this archetype has gotten a very bad rap. Her openly sexual nature and the power it gives her are too much for society to handle. In ancient times sexual union in Aphrodite's temples was considered a sacred and purifying act. Now, however, a distrust of the sexually active woman has relegated her to the status of prostitute, slut or femme fatale. There is, however, a growing goddess movement in the United States that seeks to reclaim such images of women as powerful.

The Seductive Muse's open sexuality causes her problems when she looks to get married and start a family. She often finds herself playing the role of mistress. It's hard for men to see her playing the role of wife and mother even though her youthful charm would bring a lot of love and spice into a marriage. Sex is the answer and cause of her problems.

Watch episodes of *Sex and the City* for a modern representation of this archetype as seen in the character Samantha Jones (Kim Cattrall). She isn't a prostitute, slut or femme fatale, just a beautiful woman who loves sex and doesn't care what others think about her.

What Does the Seductive Muse Care About?

✪ The Seductive Muse cares about men—at least the intimate part of relationships. She loves being in control but doesn't try to dominate men openly. She secretly manipulates them with her charm. She's an expert in body language, always seeing the hidden desires of others. She tries to awaken them in her partners and friends by bringing their repressed feelings to the surface.

✪ If she's been hurt, she can put up a wall when it comes to emotional involvement with a lover, telling herself "someone better is just around the corner."

✪ Her relationships with other women are important to her, but she seldom finds a true best friend. She wants other women to express their sexuality as openly as she does, but only other Seductive Muses can understand her intensity. At the same time she doesn't understand other archetypes. The Nurturer seems boring to her, and the Father's Daughter is too mentally focused and rigid. She lives for the moment and won't be held down by friendships with these archetypes.

✪ Although she may not admit it, she cares about being the center of attention and about being the most desired woman in the room. She loves her body and shows it off every chance she gets. Her body is part of her identity.

✪ Any form of expression can be important to her—dancing, singing or drawing. Her sexual creative energy can be channeled through these expressions, and it becomes an obsession.

In *Cabaret,* Sally Bowles (Liza Minnelli) has an impulsive nature and a desire for a life free of commitments—both traits of the Seductive Muse archetype.

What Does the Seductive Muse Fear?

✪ The Seductive Muse fears losing her sexuality, allure and creativity. It would devastate her. This can happen if she contracts a sexually transmitted disease or is assaulted. Her emotional center would be scarred for life.

✪ Rejection of any sort can be an enormous blow to her, especially if it comes from a lover. Her charm over men gives her power, and she wants to be the one to end the relationship. She's like Cleopatra in her relationship with Caesar—filled with sex, power and intrigue.

✪ Aging is terrifying to her, the end to her charm and magnetism, casting her into a lonely existence. She may never get married, but her need for people and attention is fueled by a fear of isolation. She believes youth and charm keep people around.

✪ She hates not being the center of attention but at the same time she fears that other women will hate her for this attention. Her best friendships seem to be with Amazons who are just as extroverted but also protective of her like a big sister, and with Maidens who look up to her—like Mary Ann (Dawn Wells) in *Gilligan's Island* looks up to Ginger (Tina Louise). Most women are dying to let loose and be more like her, but they don't know how and wind up becoming jealous of her. Her relationships with other Seductive Muses become competitive rather quickly.

What Motivates the Seductive Muse?

✪ Her biggest motivator is self-actualization. Whether she's publicly recognized or not she has an urge to create. There is a need deep within her soul that drives her to produce things and experience life to the fullest. Without a creative outlet she expresses this drive sexually. She's like Catherine Tramell (Sharon Stone) in *Basic Instinct*; when she's not writing she sexually plays with men and women for fun.

✪ She needs love, connection and creativity to be happy. She may have trouble seeing projects through to the end, loving the process itself more than anything. When the project ends so does the fun.

How Do Other Characters See the Seductive Muse?

✪ Some women are jealous of the attention she receives. She can see it in their eyes. How many women would be comfortable with Marilyn Monroe in the room? They don't understand the charm and magnetism she has over men and women alike. She is sexual, colorful and full of a love for life, something most women have trouble cultivating. They watch her and feel their own shortcomings.

✪ She wears alluring clothes and sometimes is ahead of the trends, possibly starting them herself. She always adds a

In biblical tales, Salome's seductive dancing led the emperor to grant her any wish.

touch of uniqueness and class to her outfits and seems to be totally perfect—hair, nails and skin all vibrant. She has an inner glow, a "star quality" about her.

Developing the Character Arc

Look at your character's main goal in your story and then at the fears you've selected to use against her. What does she need to learn to help her overcome her fear? Does she need to learn how to be by herself in nature? Does she need to turn another woman into a sexual goddess and step out of the limelight herself?

Very often the Seductive Muse just wants to be recognized for her brain instead of just her looks. She may learn that looks are temporary and superficial. She wants a true soul mate who sees her for who she is. She needs to learn to sit still and to plan for the future instead of always living in the moment.

What happened to her at an early age to make this archetype dominate her personality? Was she treated like the favored child and spoiled for her innocent alluring behavior? Did she live in a culture where women were encouraged to be open and giving? Was she sexually abused and is now acting out her abuse unconsciously by sleeping around and degrading herself?

To grow, this archetype is best paired with one of the following:

○ **The Woman's Man**—can teach her to value herself for her mind and spirit as well as her body.

○ **The Messiah**—can teach her how to channel her sexual energy to advance spiritually.

○ **The Recluse and Mystic**—can teach her how to be alone without fear of abandonment and also how to know herself deep down inside.

○ **The Amazon**—can teach her to set limits and accept discipline as a positive thing in life.

THE SEDUCTIVE MUSE
Assets:
- Loves to be the center of attention.
- Has a need to express herself.
- Is smart and creative.
- Is emotional and deeply feeling.
- Loves herself and her body in a healthy way. No eating disorders here.
- Loves to dress up and wear alluring clothes.
- Enjoys sex.

- Enjoys female friendships but sometimes feels ostracized.
- Encourages other women to be creative and sexual; inspires men.

Flaws:
- Is unable to do things alone.
- Lives for the moment, never thinking of or planning for the future.
- Falls in and out of love easily—loves 'em and leaves 'em.
- Is manipulative and flirtatious.
- Is impulsive and promiscuous.
- Is very self-focused.

The Villainous Side of the Seductive Muse: The Femme Fatale

She deliberately uses her charm to control men and get them to do things against their nature. She's the Femme Fatale who lures nice men to crime and murder. She trusts no one. She has become jaded and disappointed with life. She only values herself for her body and feels powerful when others do her bidding. Society owes her, and she is only collecting her due.

She never dirties her own hand when she can manipulate a man into doing the dirty work for her. She will push and tease men, dangling her body in front of them like a golden carrot. Any man who strives for her will end up dead or completely ruined. Watch any film noir movie to see her in action.

Things can get ugly when she turns on a lover. Blackmail is the first thing on her mind if he's married, but she'll do anything to save face if crossed. She doesn't play victim easily and would rather die than give up her looks or power. If a younger woman tries to take over her position as the center

Cleopatra preferred to commit suicide rather than give up her power. This need for power is a defining characteristic of the Femme Fatale.

of attention, watch out. In the words of Bette Davis in *All About Eve*, "Fasten your seatbelts. It's going to be a bumpy night."

She has a pattern of excessive emotionalism and attention seeking. She has a low tolerance for problems and has rapidly changing emotions behind a face that remains stoic and unreadable. She's a ticking bomb that no one knows about until she explodes. She is sensitive to criticism and overly concerned with her appearance.

She may suggest that a man do something and then withhold sex until he does it. She uses her body as a weapon. She feels that if men are stupid enough to get sucked into her web then that's their problem. No one handed her anything as a kid. She had to manipulate people and use what God gave her to survive. She trusts no one and is driven to prove she's not a piece of meat to be thrown around.

THE FEMME FATALE
- Feels she can trust no one.
- Deliberately manipulates others with her sexual promises and usually never delivers unless she has to.
- Has no morals.
- Has a kill-or-be-killed mentality.
- Is a great actress who can summon real tears on command.
- Is concerned with money and power, which equal survival to her.
- Is unfaithful.
- Doesn't take things personally when sex is involved; she can remain detached.
- No one ever knows when she speaks the truth.
- Is a chameleon who can be all things to all people.
- Uses her physical appearance to draw others into her web.
- Needs to be the center of attention.
- Has rapidly changing emotions behind a face that remains stoic and unreadable.
- Is sensitive to criticism.

Aphrodite in Action
Seductive Muse/Femme Fatale TV Heroes
Samantha Jones (Kim Cattrall) in *Sex and the City*
Kelly Bundy (Christina Applegate) in *Married With Children*
Ginger Grant (Tina Louise) in *Gilligan's Island*

Audrey Horne (Sherilyn Fenn) in *Twin Peaks*

Erika Kane (Susan Lucci) in *All My Children*

Seductive Muse/Femme Fatale Film Heroes

Catherine Tramell (Sharon Stone) in *Basic Instinct*

Elvira in *Elvira, Mistress of the Dark*

Cora Smith (Lana Turner) in *The Postman Always Rings Twice*

Vivian Ward (Julia Roberts) in *Pretty Woman*

Lana (Rebecca De Mornay) in *Risky Business*

Sally Bowles (Liza Minnelli) in *Cabaret*

Rizzo (Stockard Channing) in *Grease*

Madeleine Elster/Judy Barton (Kim Novak) in *Vertigo*

Seductive Muse/Femme Fatale Literary and Historical Heroes

Cleopatra

Delilah

Salome

Marilyn Monroe

Mary, Queen of Scots

Emma Bovary in *Madame Bovary* by Gustave Flaubert

The Lady Chablis in *Midnight in the Garden of Good and Evil* by John Berendt

Scarlett O'Hara in *Gone With the Wind* by Margaret Mitchell

Rebecca Sharp in *Vanity Fair* by William Makepeace Thackeray

Chapter 4

Artemis
The Amazon and the Gorgon

Under the glimmer of moonlight among towering forest trees, walks the goddess Artemis. Close to her side she carries with her a silver bow and arrows. She glides through the night watching over innocent young women and seeking out a challenger to polish her skill as an expert archer. She is the chief hunter to the gods, goddesses and wild animals. As she walks beneath the moon in her wilderness, her ears are ever open for the sound of a young female, human or animal, who may need her help in childbirth or need her protection from rape. With a quick temper she punishes those who offend her. She is a goddess who chooses to live without a mate, self-sufficient. With great precision and concentration, she sets her mind's eye on a goal and pursues it until the end.

The Amazon

The Amazon is a feminist. She cares more about the female cause than she cares for her own safety. She wouldn't hesitate to come to the aid of another woman or child no matter what the risk is to herself. Her friendships with women are the most important relationships she has, but they are few and far between due to her androgynous attitudes. Her masculine side is just as strong as her feminine side, which sometimes leaves her confused about where she fits in with others. She doesn't keep up with fashion trends and she doesn't value the "stay at home" or the "corporate career" woman, which most women are these days.

She is a wild woman who spends as much time in nature as possible. She's never happy living in the city for long and may become frustrated with her life until she discovers her true passion for the outdoors. The solitude of walking in the crisp night air brings her back into balance, and she is never afraid of being out alone at night.

She is an "earth mother" of sorts, taking up the causes of recycling and protecting the earth's resources. She is intuitive, instinctual and loves to travel and explore exotic places. Rose DeWitt Bukater (Kate Winslet) in *Titanic* is a caged Amazon.

What Does the Amazon Care About?

⊘ An Amazon cares deeply about the feminine, nature and the earth. There's no love lost between her and the government when they start regulating land near natural resources. She believes the earth is for everyone. No one "owns" the land, and she'll go wherever she pleases.

⊘ She looks after women and children and passionately fights patriarchy. She feels everyone deserves to be free and independent and that women are equal to men in all situations.

⊘ Competitive sports are her favorite pastime and winning is always the goal.

What Does the Amazon Fear?

⊘ The Amazon fears losing her freedom and independence. She takes great pride in being able to take care of herself. Going to prison or becoming paralyzed would kill her spirit. She places value on being self-sufficient and looks down on others who are dependent and needy, even though she comes to their aid.

⊘ Her competitive nature makes her afraid of losing, whether it's a job or a sporting event. And she especially doesn't want to lose to a man. She's afraid she'll never hear the end of it. She enjoys proving she's the equal of any man, mostly in physical ways.

In Louisa May Alcott's *Little Women,* Jo's independence and care for her sisters are examples of her Amazon characteristics.

✪ She's most afraid of being vulnerable. She would rather die than become a victim, especially of a sexual assault. Her spirit could never survive such a humiliation. She will fight to the death against any attacker, making her a force to reckon with.

✪ She isn't afraid of her own death but afraid of other women and children dying when she could've helped them. She finds her identity in being the rescuer.

✪ She's afraid of other women alienating her for her masculine attributes. She's not into makeup and hairstyles. She's a "let's go out and tear up the town" kind of gal. Female friendships are important to her but it's hard to find other Amazons to go out with. She winds up having more male friends than female friends.

What Motivates the Amazon?

✪ Survival is her biggest motivator. She loves being left alone in the wilds to fend for herself. Her relationship with wild animals and nature makes her instinctual and primal, and she can take this instinct to the boardroom to battle men for position and power.

✪ Getting behind a cause she cares deeply about invigorates her. She needs to be challenged and stimulated, otherwise boredom sets in along with depression. She admires all the women who fought for the right to vote, risking their safety for the greater good.

✪ Saving a woman's or child's life gives her purpose and enormous self-esteem. She's like Xena rescuing Gabrielle. She feels like a big sister to all women, a martyr for the female cause as well as environmental causes.

How Do Other Characters See the Amazon?

✪ She doesn't think too much about her clothes. She loves to wear loose-fitting clothes that she can move around in easily. In Greek mythology Artemis asks her father Zeus for a short tunic to wear, not because it's sexy, but because it will allow her to run fast.

✪ Her athletic figure is sometimes alluring but also intimidating to both men and women.

✪ Other people sometimes see her as cold and totally absorbed in her own tasks. She has an ability to focus so intently on her goals that it leaves her looking distant and aloof at times, but when she's enjoying nature she plays like a child. She never wears a watch because time is meaningless to her.

Developing the Character Arc

Look at your character's main goal in your story and then at the fears you have selected to use against her. What does she need to learn to help her overcome her fear? Does she need to raise a child? Does she need to use her intellect and come

Joan of Arc's willingness to fight for a cause she believed in is typical of the Amazon archetype.

to terms with city life? Does she have to come to terms with not being able to save someone?

Very often an Amazon wants a place of her own with a small group of close friends who come and go. She wants to be recognized for her efforts and all the help she gives. She needs to learn to trust men most of all.

What happened to her at an early age to make this archetype dominate her personality? Was she raised without a mother and sisters, making her take on attributes from her father? Was her mother an Amazon? Did she play sports instead of dress up? Did she watch as someone she loved was hurt? Was there a heroic female character she idolized and wanted to be, like Wonder Woman?

To grow, this archetype is best paired with one of the following:

❖ **The Protector**—can teach her to trust others to help her.

❖ **The Fool and The Maiden**—can teach her about fun, adventure and how to be easygoing.

❖ **The Nurturer**—can teach her the value of giving birth and being a mother.

THE AMAZON

Assets:

- Loves to be outside with animals and nature.
- Prefers female friendships to male, but often winds up with more male friends.
- Values women and children.
- Is a feminist even if she doesn't say she is in your story.
- Is unafraid to be out alone at night.
- Is willing and able to fight to the death to defend herself.
- Stands up for her causes.
- Prefers function to style when it comes to her clothes and appearance.
- Wants to be self-sufficient.
- Prefers to live with a man instead of marrying him.

Flaws:

- Can be very opinionated and thickheaded.
- Puts blinders on; everything but the goal at hand is forgotten.
- Can become irrational because of her need to win at all costs.
- Can be boastful.

• May take on the traits of her aggressors in order to feel equal to them.

The Villainous Side of the Amazon: The Gorgon

As a villain she would do anything to come to the aid of another woman, even if it meant killing an innocent man by mistake. Her rage at injustice is swift, merciless and sometimes aimed at the wrong person.

She is Medusa, the Gorgon, the woman of fury and rage, especially if she's been violated. She can turn deadly when she feels threatened and is capable of using extremely physical means to express her anger. Most men don't expect a woman to be as strong as her rage can make her.

She'll fight to the death like a mother lion protecting her cubs. In her fury she won't think about her own life and survival. She sees red and fights like someone who struggles for air; nothing else matters. All thoughts of democracy, diplomacy, and right and wrong are irrelevant to her. She'll be avenged at all costs. If her cause is just she feels the Goddess will support her, make her efforts successful and forgive her for her brutality.

She's antisocial with irresponsible behavior that lacks morals and ethics. She exhibits unlawful reckless behavior, refusing to conform to social norms. She seems to have no emotional reactions and shows no remorse toward horrific events. She is physically aggressive, erratic and irritable, and disregards the safety of herself and of others.

She feels justified in her actions because she feels basic rights have been violated. She wants to enable women to be strong and defend themselves at all costs. Sometimes one person is unjustly killed but she believes if it saves many then so be it. She doesn't care if she becomes just like the aggressor she hates. She believes in fighting fire with fire. She doesn't care what anyone else thinks, and she'll destroy herself before she lets anyone else do it for her. She feels she is the master of her life and destiny.

THE GORGON

- Is instinctual and shows no remorse.
- Wants instant gratification and justice.
- Is blind with fury and rage.
- Creates extremely emotional reactions out of proportion to offense.
- Isn't levelheaded.
- Acts as a dictator, dispensing justice.
- Believes truth and law have no place in the heat of battle.
- Will sacrifice herself to get an enemy.
- Usually reacts from repressed trauma or years of abuse.
- Exhibits reckless behavior.
- Is aggressive, erratic and irritable.

Diana in Action
Amazon/Gorgon TV Heroes

Buffy Summers (Sarah Michelle Gellar) in *Buffy the Vampire Slayer*

Xena (Lucy Lawless) in *Xena: Warrior Princess*

Dr. Michaela Quinn (Jane Seymour) in *Dr. Quinn, Medicine Woman*

Nikita (Peta Wilson) in *La Femme Nikita*

Amazon/Gorgon Film Heroes

Rose DeWitt Bukater (Kate Winslet) in *Titanic*

Lieutenant Ellen L. Ripley (Sigourney Weaver) in *Alien*

Louise Sawyer (Susan Sarandon) in *Thelma & Louise*

Karen Silkwood (Meryl Streep) in *Silkwood*

Captain Karen Emma Walden (Meg Ryan) in *Courage Under Fire*

Sarah Connor (Linda Hamilton) in *The Terminator*

Gracie Hart (Sandra Bullock) in *Miss Congeniality*

Amazon/Gorgon Literary and Historical Heroes

Wonder Woman

Joan of Arc

Queen Boudica

Fa Mu Lan in *The Woman Warrior: Memoirs of a Girlhood Among Ghosts* by Maxine Hong Kingston

Sal in *The Beach* by Alex Garland

Jo March in *Little Women* by Louisa May Alcott

Helen Schlegel in *Howards End* by E.M. Forster

Scout in *To Kill a Mockingbird* by Harper Lee

Lucy in *The Lion, the Witch and the Wardrobe* by C.S. Lewis

Idgie Threadgoode in *Fried Green Tomatoes at the Whistle Stop Cafe* by Fannie Flagg

Anne Shirley in *Anne of Green Gables* by Lucy Maud Montgomery

Chapter 5

Athena

The Father's Daughter and the Backstabber

As mysterious as an owl in the dark night air, the goddess Athena hovers proudly over the great library and the victorious battlefield. She will not dirty her hands in battle but will remain at the side of her chosen heroic soldier, helping him to win the war. She offers him strength, power and knowledge as well as her undying loyalty. She carries a shield of armor in one hand and an image of the goddess Nike in the other for Nike is the symbol of victory. Born from her father's head, she has no mother and no room for female companions of any kind. She is smart and takes full control of her emotions.

The Father's Daughter

The Father's Daughter doesn't care much for fighting the good fight for women's causes like the Amazon does. She may argue against the female cause, siding with men to prove she's on their side thereby gaining their admiration. She feels she is the exceptional woman—"Other women can't do this," she thinks, "but I can because I'm the exception."

She forms alliances with strong men who can help her achieve her goals. She doesn't sleep with them but instead develops friendships with them as "one of the boys." She's the type of woman who is eagerly allowed into the male workplace for she is always loyal to the strong men she unites with in the battlefield of business.

She is smart and a very strategic thinker, never allowing her emotions to sway her into making the wrong decision. She hates the wild untamed wilderness, preferring a fast-paced city

Queen Elizabeth's steel-minded resolve and dedication to her father's causes make her an example of a historical Father's Daughter.

life. She likes things she can control but also loves the challenge of learning new things, especially those related to the mind and the business world. She uses brains over instinct and can focus on her own goals just like the Amazon. As a goddess she oversees crafts as well as warfare, for both take patience and concentration. She has the strength to be professional and to be a gifted student. She is very inquisitive and resourceful in a crisis but doesn't trust others to get things done for her and often takes on everything herself.

Without the skills or opportunities for business she will rally behind her husband's career as if it were her own. Watch out if he ever tries to leave her. She would be most upset at the loss of being involved with his job more than anything.

Lieutenant Jordan "L.T." O'Neil (Demi Moore) in *G.I. Jane* is a Father's Daughter, not an Amazon, because she fights to become just like a man and prove she is as good as a man. An Amazon would retain and value her female essence. Jordan tries to fit into the boys' club as a male. Her words, manners, actions and values are very male by the end of the film, and she sacrifices herself for their approval several times. An Amazon like Xena would never care so much about fitting in, and in the film *Courage Under Fire* we see a heroic Amazon woman, Captain Karen Emma Walden (Meg Ryan), who retains her female essence throughout the film. She has no problem with feelings and tears.

What Does the Father's Daughter Care About?

❂ Her name says it all—she cares about aligning herself with powerful men and supporting patriarchy. She wants to be accepted by men as one of their own so she can get ahead in her career. Getting into the old boys' network is a major career stepping-stone for her.

❂ She only cares how men view her. Women can say what they want of her but she feels they usually wind up admiring her for her accomplishments.

❂ She loves to win, or more importantly, to see her team win. She'll go to great lengths to see this happen—she's a real team player.

❂ She wants to study and learn new things, to broaden her mind.

❂ She likes to travel to distant lands but never without staying in a luxury hotel. She never does anything she can hire someone else to do for her. She has a busy schedule.

What Does the Father's Daughter Fear?

❂ The Father's Daughter fears female friendship because it reminds her of her own femaleness, which she tries to suppress. She sees women as the weaker sex and fights everyday to prove she's not weak.

❂ She can handle losing a battle or two but is terrified of losing the war. Such a loss of control is devastating.

❂ She needs to remain in the city. Going out into the wil-

Like the Father's Daughter archetype, Margo Channing (Bette Davis) in *All About Eve* is strong, stubborn and proud. She is a natural leader.

derness would just starve her desire to learn from books. She needs to see that nature has a lot to teach her as well as books do, but she just doesn't resonate with it.

What Motivates the Father's Daughter?

✪ The need to know, understand and belong are strong motivators for her. She wants desperately to fit in with the boys and prove she's better than most women.

✪ Any challenge that allows her to use her strength in strategizing will grab her attention. She won't tolerate anything disorderly.

✪ She needs to be self-sufficient and independent, but she likes to know there's a powerful man nearby to fall on "just in case." She likes how the goddess Athena helped Achilles reach his goal but also wanted him to be of service to her.

✪ Competition is one of her great passions, especially when it involves sharing the risk within a team so she doesn't have to be the only one to fail. If she loses, the entire team loses and she won't be left alone to pick up the pieces.

How Do Others See the Father's Daughter?

✪ She's neat and professional in appearance. Even when she's at home alone she wears nice neat clothing; it may not be the most comfortable thing to wear, but appearance counts.

✪ To others she seems unemotional because she's always cool and calm in a crisis. She appears to be calculating something behind intense eyes.

✪ She has a hard time letting loose in front of others. Her home is the only place where she can truly relax. She has some playful games and hobbies hidden in her closet. She enjoys indoor activities best.

Developing the Character Arc

Look at your character's main goal in the story and then at the fears you've selected to use against her. What does she need to learn to help her overcome her fear? Does she need to learn how to live in a remote town in order to save her law firm? Does she need to lose an important account so she can save her boss's career?

Very often a Father's Daughter needs to get back to nature to ease her stress and regain her health. She needs to learn that being a woman is OK, and she doesn't have to do everything herself. Perhaps being "one of the boys" isn't that important. See the film *Baby Boom* as an example of the Father's Daughter who has to give up her career, move to a house in the country and raise her dead relative's child.

What happened to her at an early age to make this archetype

dominate her personality? Did she see her mother trampled on by men and swear she'd never be that weak? Did her father have all the control in the family? Was she forced to stay inside and play alone as a child, going into her head and out of her body?

To grow, this archetype is best paired with one of the following:

✪ The Artist—can teach her about creativity and letting go in the moment.

✪ The Seducer—can open her sexuality and teach her how to have personal relationships with men.

✪ The Destroyer—can teach her about raw female power.

✪ The Scorned Woman—hates other women, such as mistresses, so much she can be an example of how ridiculous it is to hate all women.

✪ The Matriarch—can show her female power within the family and teach her traditional values.

THE FATHER'S DAUGHTER

Assets:

- Loves to be in the city.
- Prefers male friendships to female.
- Values work and career above all else.
- Is willing to do anything for the team.
- Is self-reliant.
- Always dresses for success even when home alone.
- Is very smart and intellectual.
- Is very confident and self-assured.

Flaws:

- Is an avid supporter of patriarchy.
- Gets upset with other women who complain about inequality.

- Is only attracted to powerful men.
- Is a workaholic.
- Is always strategizing.
- Is unable to fully express her feminine side and be in touch with her body. Dancing is hard for her.

The Villainous Side of the Father's Daughter: The Backstabber

As a villain the Father's Daughter will trample others to reach her goals. She can use her calculating, strategic mind to outsmart anyone, and her alliances with powerful men allow her to do this. Sometimes these men take advantage of her loyalty.

Her rage is great when she learns a man she trusted has betrayed her. While the Amazon woman expects it, the Father's Daughter feels devastated by it because she learns she isn't "one of the boys" like she thought she was. She spends her whole life trying to fit in with them.

Her whole identity can become wrapped up in her career. Losing it is like death to her. She'll become disloyal before she lets that happen. She'll use her femininity to play the innocent woman routine and later stab a colleague in the back.

She'll also vehemently fight a woman who fights for women's rights. She doesn't want to admit that the playing field isn't equal for all because that means it's not equal for her. She wants to distance herself from her feminine side and all its weaknesses as she sees it.

She has unwarranted fears that others are out to get her. She's preoccupied with doubts about the loyalty and trustworthiness of others and is unable to confide in them for fear that what she says will be used against her. She can't relax and is unable to collaborate with colleagues. She becomes suspicious of everyone and detaches herself from the group. Her sense of humor completely disappears.

She doesn't understand what's wrong with wanting to be successful, powerful and on top. She enjoys the company of men more than women but always has a trump card waiting in the wings to revenge any colleague who betrays her.

THE BACKSTABBER

- Feels trapped.
- Plays off of the sweet little woman stereotype perfectly when it suits her.
- Thinks of herself first.
- Has no problem destroying another's life or career.
- Relies on the kindness of strangers in her time of need.
- Lets others feel good about helping her so they let their guard down.
- Is an expert liar until her buttons are pushed and she lashes out, spilling her true feelings.
- Is paranoid and feels that others are plotting against her.
- Has trouble relaxing.
- Can't confide in or collaborate with colleagues.
- Detaches herself from the group.

Athena in Action
Father's Daughter/Backstabber TV Heroes

Captain Kathryn Janeway (Kate Mulgrew) in *Star Trek: Voyager*

Dana Scully (Gillian Anderson) in *The X-Files*

Murphy Brown (Candice Bergen) in *Murphy Brown*

Prue Halliwell (Shannon Doherty) in *Charmed*

Father's Daughter/Backstabber Film Heroes

Elizabeth I (Cate Blanchett) in *Elizabeth*

Lieutenant Jordan "L.T." O'Neil (Demi Moore) in *G.I. Jane*
J.C. Wiatt (Diane Keaton) in *Baby Boom*
Katherine Parker (Sigourney Weaver) in *Working Girl*
Margo Channing (Bette Davis) in *All About Eve*
Loretta Castorini (Cher) in *Moonstruck*

Father's Daughter/Backstabber Literary and Historical Heroes

Matilda, Countess of Tuscany
Kate in *The Taming of the Shrew* by William Shakespeare
Beatrice in *Much Ado About Nothing* by William
    Shakespeare
Lady Macbeth in *Macbeth* by William Shakespeare
Bernie Harris in *Waiting to Exhale* by Terry McMillan
Kinsey Millhone in books by Sue Grafton
Clarice Starling in *The Silence of the Lambs* by Thomas
    Harris
Karen Sisco in *Out of Sight* by Elmore Leonard

Chapter 6

Demeter

The Nurturer and the Overcontrolling Mother

Wandering the cold winter streets at night, Demeter searches for her abducted daughter Persephone. Ceasing to eat, drink and sleep, she is consumed by the empty space next to her where her daughter walked at her side. Her tears of depression cast a chill over the fields of grain. Nothing grows across the land she walks on. Winter takes over with her every step until her beloved daughter is returned to her. Only then will grain grow and spring come to the land. She cares not for herself but only for her child.

The Nurturer

Demeter is the nurturing mother, but it isn't necessary for this archetype to have children to be a nurturer. A sense of duty to help others is what's essential. The Nurturer refused all of the superficial gifts sent to her by other gods to persuade her to accept her daughter's abduction, rape and forced marriage to Hades. She wants her child back, and nothing else matters. With her child gone a part of her is missing. She is youthful when she lives through the life of her child.

The Nurturer has dreamed of having children for most of her life, and when she has them they become her life. If she's unable to have children or if she's looking for the right "father" to come along, she channels her energy into helping and caring for others. She can often be found in the nursing and healing professions.

She forms friendships with other Demeter women who see value in motherhood and service. They can spend hours talking

In *Stella Dallas*, the title character (Barbara Stanwyck) is such a devoted mother, she sacrifices her own desires and gives up all ties to her daughter in order to help better her daughter's social status.

about the latest healing techniques or ways to raise children.

Her identity is wrapped up in her children or those she cares for. They give her life purpose and meaning. She can nurture many people through her work in a charitable organization, help animals at a shelter, care for her own family, help a stranger on the street, be there for a close friend or lover, care for her students, or help the masses with a creative project like a self-help book.

What Does the Nurturer Care About?

❂ The Nurturer cares about the welfare of her children whether there's danger present or not. She has a tendency to put others ahead of herself—a martyr of sorts—but no one comes before the one in her care especially if it's a child. She would sacrifice an entire town if it meant saving her child.

In the fairy tale, Beauty's motherly concern for the Beast (a Recluse archetype) makes her an example of a Nurturer.

⊘ When things are going well she cares about providing for the entire group and bestows amazing gifts to people she hardly knows. The sick people she cares for call her an angel.

⊘ She cares about charities and volunteers when she has free time.

⊘ She sometimes lives on eggshells, making sure everyone else is happy before she examines how she feels.

What Does the Nurturer Fear?

⊘ The Nurturer fears losing the person in her care. Her whole identity and reason to live depends upon caring for another. It makes her angry when someone accuses her of destroying the independence of the person in her care in order to protect him from a danger that may not exist.

⊘ She fears not being there to save her child. If anything happens she'll take all the guilt upon herself and fall into a devastating depression. She can't help it. Grief consumes her, and she makes everyone else around her suffer.

⊘ She couldn't stand it if her child or patient left. She needs to be needed and is a prime candidate for "empty-nest syndrome."

⊘ She's not into self-analysis because she's afraid of her own thoughts and emotions. She hates quiet time because she doesn't like to think about her "stuff." She'd rather be busy with anything else to avoid it.

What Motivates the Nurturer?

⊘ Love and belonging are strong motivators for her. She likes being connected with someone. Give her a family and she'll bestow gifts upon them as long as they allow her to care for them. She would definitely adopt a sick child.

⊘ Motherhood and nurturing give her a reason to live. She'll do anything to save this precious relationship. Demeter was very strong as she was able to denounce all the other gods and hold fast to her goal of getting her daughter back. The Nurturer admires that part of the story.

How Do Other Characters See the Nurturer?

⊘ Some see her as dependent, needy and passive aggressive.

⊘ She tends to take on many tasks at once, trying to please so many people, overwhelming herself.

⊘ She's not concerned with being sexy and doesn't care much for the latest fashions. She can be a very beautiful woman but seems not to realize it.

Developing the Character Arc

Look at your character's main goal in the story and then at the fears you've selected to use against her. What does she need to learn to overcome her fear? Does she need to learn to let go of her children and find a career? Does she need to stand up for herself and speak her mind without worrying about hurting others? Does she need to let her children grow up and leave home?

Very often the Nurturer needs to let go of her attachment to others and find her own identity. She needs to learn that she can take care of herself and that being alone sometimes can be refreshing. A hobby such as yoga and writing can help her find self-love.

What happened to her at an early age to make this archetype dominate her personality? Was her mother not there for her and now she wants to make up for that by being there for others? Did she have to help raise her siblings as a child? Was she given dolls and told being a mother is the greatest thing in the world? Was there a special woman in her life, like a teacher, who helped her and now she wants to give back?

To grow, this archetype is best paired with one of the following:

❂ **The Woman's Man**—can nurture her back and show her what it feels like to be in an equal relationship with another.

❂ **The Recluse**—can teach her the value of being alone and knowing herself.

❂ **The Gorgon**—can teach her the harsh realities of life and how to stop people from walking all over her.

❂ **The Mystic**—can teach her self-love.

THE NURTURER
Assets:

- Spends a lot of time with her children or students or patients, whoever is in her care.
- Puts others ahead of herself.

- Is driven to help people.
- Is wonderful to be around.
- Is extremely helpful.
- Is a great listener.
- Is committed to her family.
- Is generous.
- Enjoys staying home most of the time.

Flaws:

- Finds her sole identity is wrapped up in helping or saving others.
- Worries constantly about her children.
- Is self-sacrificing and takes on too many projects at one time because she can't say no.
- Takes things her family says personally.
- Needs someone to care for.

The Villainous Side of the Nurturer: The Overcontrolling Mother

As a villain the Nurturer would probably kidnap someone else's baby just to have someone to take care of. She would steal someone else's creative project to be looked upon as helpful to society.

She would manipulate another person into letting her help them by taking over their life, like Annie Wilkes (Kathy Bates) does in *Misery*.

She's the mother who poisons her child so she can bring her to the hospital and receives attention for all the hard work she's doing to care for her child. She's the mother who projects her own disappointments onto her daughter so she won't leave home and be independent. She's the master of inflicting guilt upon others.

She does everything with the thought that people need her. She thinks others can't live without her, but in reality she can't live without them. She believes she's helping people but what she's actually doing is occupying herself with other people's lives in an effort to avoid her own.

She's a very dependent person who can't function without someone else around to keep her company and provide direction.

She feels devastated or helpless when relationships end and is preoccupied with fears of being abandoned. Her lack of self-confidence makes it impossible for her to do things on her own. She cares for others in an effort to make sure others will be there to care for her. She feels helpless when left alone.

She feels she has given up her entire life to raise her children. She sacrificed everything for them. She wants respect and obedience.

THE OVERCONTROLLING MOTHER

- Feels like others are trying to toss her aside and abandon her.
- Thinks others can't survive without her when she's the one who can't survive without them.
- Will hurt others for their own good.
- Butts in when not wanted.
- Uses guilt to control others.
- Exaggerates when hurt or in need.
- Does things not asked of her to seem helpful.
- Seems genuinely nice once in a while to throw others off balance.
- Lacks self-confidence.
- Can't do anything alone.

Demeter in Action

Nurturer/Overcontrolling Mother TV Heroes

Carol Ann Brady (Florence Henderson) in *The Brady Bunch*

Daphne Moon (Jane Leeves) in *Frasier*

Marie Barone (Doris Roberts) in *Everybody Loves Raymond*

Piper Halliwell (Holly Marie Combs) in *Charmed*

June Cleaver (Barbara Billingsley) in *Leave It to Beaver*

Nurturer/Overcontrolling Mother Film Heroes

Carol Connelly (Helen Hunt) in *As Good As It Gets*

Stella Dallas (Barbara Stanwyck) in *Stella Dallas*

M'Lynn Eatenton (Sally Field) in *Steel Magnolias*

Dorothy Boyd (Renée Zellweger) in *Jerry Maguire*

There are a number of classic films where the female character is relegated to the house, caring for the men. These characters are prevalent in Westerns. You can see them waiting in doorways, watching over the men and taking care of their wounds.

Nurturer/Overcontrolling Mother Literary and Historical Heroes

Florence Nightingale

Mother Teresa

Beauty in *Beauty and the Beast*

Mary Poppins in *Mary Poppins* by Pamela L. Travers

Widow Douglas in *The Adventures of Huckleberry Finn* by Mark Twain

Meg March in *Little Women* by Louisa May Alcott

Nurse in *Romeo and Juliet* by William Shakespeare

Miss Emma and Tante Lou in *A Lesson Before Dying* by Ernest J. Gaines

Francesca Johnson in *The Bridges of Madison County* by Robert James Waller

Elinor Dashwood in *Sense and Sensibility* by Jane Austen

Grandmother in *100 Years of Solitude* by Gabriel García Márquez

Ruth in *Fried Green Tomatoes at the Whistle Stop Cafe* by Fannie Flagg

Sethe in *Beloved* by Toni Morrison

Annie Wilkes in *Misery* by Stephen King

Sally Owens in *Practical Magic* by Alice Hoffman

Chapter 7

Hera
The Matriarch and the Scorned Woman

Hera the powerful goddess of marriage and fertility spills forth the stars of the Milky Way seeding the earth. Heracles' (Hercules) name means "glory to Hera," a testament to her immense power. When Zeus took a liking to her she was able to resist him until he promised to marry her. He later betrayed her causing her to become vengeful. Marriage vows are sacred to her, and she would not leave Zeus or give up on their partnership. She now uses her power to hold the family of gods together, dispensing justice and giving advice.

The Matriarch

The Matriarch is the woman in charge. She sees to the needs of her family and demands respect in return. She needs her family just as much as she would have them believe they need her. She has no identity outside of her role as wife and mother, but unlike the Nurturer she is extremely strong, resourceful and tough skinned. She doesn't take it well if her husband is unfaithful, and she will not just sit by and ignore the wrongs done to her.

She's a very strong and committed woman. No other archetype can be as faithful and loving a partner as the Matriarch. She'll never leave a family member or colleague no matter what happens in life. She can be very supportive and giving when she wants to be, and she expects the same in return. She's the one everyone looks to for advice.

Her wedding day is the most important day of her life. She wants her wedding day to last forever. The sense of inner fulfillment she feels as she walks down the aisle is addictive.

All eyes are on her, the center of attention and the object of admiration. Her husband becomes her life, and she sees their union as entering into a legal agreement with one another. It's as if they are forming a corporation. She wants to be the perfect wife, but she doesn't do it to make her husband happy; she does it to make herself happy. She takes pride in running a strong household.

Without a family of her own she'll put all of her energy and strength into starting her own company and creating a surrogate family with employees.

What Does the Matriarch Care About?

❂ The Matriarch cares about becoming a wife and may feel incomplete without her husband and family when she is married. Marriage brings her prestige and her wedding day is the happiest day of her life. Wedding vows are sacred to her and she takes commitment seriously.

❂ She wants to keep her extended family together and to be in constant control of them even if they no longer live in her house. She feels they need her help.

❂ She loves to make plans and host get-togethers. Everyone had better show up, too, or she'll never let them forget it. Nothing is more important than coming to a family party.

❂ Her husband is her identity; family comes second. She dotes on her children and may take over when the grandchildren come. A daughter-in-law often becomes upset with her for the strong child-rearing advice she gives. She means her advice as law.

What Does the Matriarch Fear?

❂ The Matriarch fears never getting married and never having children. When she does get married she fears the loss

In *Terms of Endearment* Aurora Greenway's (Shirley MacLaine) desire to control her daughter's life makes her an example of a Matriarch.

of her husband and will stick with him through good and bad no matter what. At any cost she'll keep her marriage together. If she didn't have a family she would strive to hold her company together at all costs.

❂ She's terrified of growing old and of being alone. She dreads the day her children will try to leave home as well as the days her husband is away on business. She doesn't know what to do with herself.

❂ She fears losing control when it comes to her children, but she hides it well. She's a fighter and will fight to save any child who has taken up drugs and needs a strong person to help. She can't help it if this child feels obligated to her later in life.

What Motivates the Matriarch?

❂ Love, belonging and respect are strong motivators for the Matriarch. She wants a family as well as a sense of unconditional love and support. She may have put a lot of work into her husband's career, and she wants to be recognized along with him. If he ever receives an award he had better thank her in his speech!

✪ Marriage and an expensive wedding are her goals. After the nuptials, she wants to be involved in all the other family weddings in her extended family. She frequently butts in and makes demands, telling everyone how things should be done.

How Do Other Characters See the Matriarch?

✪ She always stands tall and strong, holding her head high even in the face of insult.

✪ She dresses in whatever style suits her husband's image so she can be seen as dedicated to his career. His career is her career.

✪ Once in a while she's caught standing in the shadows listening to her children's private conversations in an effort to keep an eye on them. She can't bear to have anything happening under her nose without prior knowledge.

✪ She seems inapproachable, like she could easily yell at you or laugh at you. She doesn't want her children thinking they can pull one over on her. She's always right; her word is law.

✪ Her strength makes her the rock everyone leans on in the family.

Developing the Character Arc

Look at your character's main goal in the story and then at the fears you've selected to use against her. What does she need to learn to help her overcome her fear? Does she need to learn how to live on her own? Does she need to learn how to deal with her husband's death and run his business? Does she need to deal with a sickness and get plenty of rest, giving up her control of the family?

Very often a Matriarch needs to learn how to commit to herself as much as she commits to her husband. Once married she gives up who she was to become the perfect wife. Everything she does is for or with her husband. She needs to realize that happiness found inside someone else can only lead to sorrow.

What happened to her at an early age to make this archetype dominate her personality? Was her mother's every move controlled by her father, and she swore never to live like that? Was she raised to be perfect, putting on an act for all the neighbors? Did her family fall apart when she was young?

To grow, this archetype is best paired with one of the following:

✪ **The Dictator**—steals control from her and upsets the family system.

✪ **The Fool and The Maiden**—show her youth, love, spontaneity and letting go of control.

✪ **The Mystic**—can teach her how to look inside herself to find out who she really is.

✪ **The Father's Daughter**—can teach her about having her own career and how to be a team player instead of a dictator.

THE MATRIARCH

Assets:

- Loves to spend time with her family, even if they drive her crazy.
- Enjoys entertaining.
- Enjoys planning parties and get-togethers for the family.
- Is very committed to her marriage.
- Dreams about her wedding day often.
- Will start a business to run like a surrogate family if she doesn't have a family of her own.

Flaws:

- Depends on her husband's or friends' love for happiness.
- Drops her friendships when she finds Mr. Right.
- Spies and invades her children's privacy in order to keep tabs on them.
- Sees her identity as wrapped up in her family.
- Puts her husband's image and career above her own.
- Can be obsessive in her need for order.

The Villainous Side of the Matriarch: The Scorned Woman

As a villain, the Matriarch's rage and power come out when she feels abandoned by her husband or family. If her husband has an affair no one near her is safe against the anger and revenge brewing inside her. She'll most likely take out her feelings on the other woman before taking it out on her husband. Her identity is so wrapped up in her husband that she has to believe it was the other woman's fault and that the marriage is salvageable. She's the one in charge, and she'll take control of her husband again.

Her life means nothing without a "family" of some sort for her to run. She needs to be in control of things. Chaos isn't acceptable to her. She can justify any action taken to preserve the integrity of her family.

She's inflexible, impulsive and unpredictable at times. Her moods fluctuate as she goes to great lengths to avoid real or imagined abandonment. She's uncertain about her long-term goals, career choices and her own identity. She feels empty and can become irritable.

She has passive-aggressive tendencies and will tell family members that it's OK if they do something she disapproves of, but her actions show them just the opposite. She may even attempt suicide or self-mutilation to gain attention.

She feels she's done everything for her family and they owe her their loyalty. She controls what goes on and if they don't like it it's too bad. No one leaves the family unit, especially not with a smile. Betrayal is the worst type of offense as far as she's concerned. She'd rather have her husband ruin himself before he ruins their sacred union. She'd rather see him dead.

THE SCORNED WOMAN

- Fears being abandoned by her husband or family.
- Is enmeshed with her husband as if they're one person. She can't see him for who he really is.
- Fights for control.
- Will do anything to save face.
- Keeps family problems hidden from others. Her children may not receive the help they need as a result.
- Exhibits passive/aggressive behavior.
- Is impulsive.
- Is uncertain about her own identity.
- May have suicidal tendencies—at least for attention.
- Can be irritable and moody.

Hera in Action
Matriarch/Scorned Woman TV Heroes

Roseanne Conner (Roseanne) in *Roseanne*
Monica Geller (Courtney Cox-Arquette) in *Friends*
Lois Wilkerson (Jane Kaczmarek) in *Malcolm in the Middle*

Matriarch/Scorned Woman Film Heroes

Brenda Cushman (Bette Midler) in *The First Wives Club*
Aurora Greenway (Shirley MacLaine) in *Terms of*

Endearment

Joan Crawford (Faye Dunaway) in *Mommie Dearest*

Carolyn Burnham (Annette Bening) in *American Beauty*

Ruth (Roseanne) in *She-Devil*

Matriarch/Scorned Woman Literary and Historical Heroes

Gertrude in *Hamlet* by William Shakespeare

Mrs. Compson in *The Sound and the Fury* by William Faulkner

Ingrid in *White Oleander* by Janet Fitch

Viviane in *Mists of Avalon* by Marion Zimmer Bradley

Lauren Olamina in *Parable of the Sower* by Octavia E. Butler

Alldera in *The Furies* by Suzy McKee Charnas

Mrs. Bennet in *Pride and Prejudice* by Jane Austen

Nurse Ratched in *One Flew Over the Cuckoo's Nest* by Ken Kesey

Chapter 8

Hestia
The Mystic and the Betrayer

Behind the flickering light of the hearth fire, Hestia blesses a home with feminine compassion and family unity. Her spirit brings joy, peace and happiness to all those in her presence. In the quiet of the night she meditates near an open window, sharing in the joys of the nighttime creatures that wander the woods as everyone else lays sleeping. She sits for hours reflecting on the inner journey of her mind, forever at peace no matter what the world brings to her doorstep.

The Mystic

Hestia is the woman of peace and mysticism. She loves to be alone with her thoughts and finds bliss in solitude. Her calm nature and quiet disposition leave her a mystery to all who meet her. How does she live without any stress?

She graces a home and performs everyday tasks with ease and pleasure. She finds honor in baking the bread families will eat. No amount of feminist discourse could ever make her feel inferior to other women who have high-powered careers. Her mind isn't easily manipulated; she was one of few goddesses able to resist the lure of Aphrodite into sex and marriage. She is at one with herself and proud of her choices. She'd choose the spiritual life of a nun before choosing marriage or external earthly desires.

She sometimes plays in the mystical realm with meditation, shamanism and divination. Her internal world is rich, and her sensitivity is extreme. She can feel the thoughts and emotions of others, which gives her great compassion but also makes her wary of public places.

The title character in *Annie Hall,* played by Diane Keaton, is a good example of the Mystic archetype; she's a free spirit who lives in her own world.

What Does the Mystic Care About?

✪ The Mystic cares about simplicity. Give her a nice home base that provides space for her to be herself, and she'll do anything to protect it. She's gentle mannered—but don't invade her quiet space! She needs room to be creative; a studio or garden is perfect.

○ She flourishes in a house where she can perform all of the household chores alone. She never wants a maid.

○ She doesn't have a strong desire to have children. She loves solitude and probably wouldn't mind being in prison as much as an Amazon woman would.

○ She takes her time in everything she does. She performs one task at a time with joy and concentration in each step. No task is beneath her and time is of no consequence.

○ Recycling and being "earth conscious" is important to her but she doesn't preach to others. She loves to be in nature and mixing herbs is a favorite pastime.

What Does the Mystic Fear?

○ The Mystic strives to overcome her fears but isn't always successful. She fears not having a place to call her own where she can be herself and escape from other people's drama.

○ She's fine with having someone else provide for her but she's somewhat uneasy that her ability to do what she wants depends on another person.

○ Losing her home or sanctuary would devastate her, but she knows she can make a home wherever she goes. To the Mystic, home truly is where the heart is.

○ Anything that takes away her privacy and her solitude is her enemy.

○ She deeply fears being in a large group of people because she's so sensitive; she feels the emotions of others and is overwhelmed in public places. She does her grocery shopping at midnight to avoid crowds.

○ She hates being in the spotlight and stays as far away from competition as possible. She doesn't like to see someone else lose on her account. She feels everyone should be honored for his or her efforts.

What Motivates the Mystic?

✪ The aesthetic need for balance—a sense of order in life, a sense of being connected with something greater than herself—is what drives her. She has a spiritual need to connect or create. She knows she's not alone on earth and sometimes senses the life forces around her.

✪ The reward of being left alone, having free time and obtaining security are great motivators. She'll do anything to sustain a quiet and calm home life. She'd rather fix her own faucet than call a plumber.

✪ The plight of others can sometimes motivate her into action and to taking up a cause. She believes everyone has their own karma to bear.

How Do Other Characters See the Mystic?

✪ Others see her as quiet, calm, unhurried and definitely not a multitasker.

✪ She has great patience and often listens to other people's problems for hours at a time even if they're not quick to return the favor. Some may see her as a pushover or a gullible woman, but beneath the surface is an understanding woman with wisdom to share. A lot goes on behind her eyes, but most people don't realize it.

✪ She usually wears clothes for simple comfort, not to stay with trends. She likes wearing thrift store clothing that shows her unique earthy style and frugal sense of recycling.

Developing the Character Arc

Look at your character's main goal in the story and then at the fears you've selected to use against her. What can she learn to overcome her fear? Does she need to learn how to stand up for herself? Does she need to speak in public in order to save her home? Does she want to get married but is afraid of commitment?

Very often a Mystic needs to learn to be assertive or her needs aren't met. She needs to go out into the world and experience life. She needs to learn that to be in love doesn't mean she has to lose her identity, which is why she stays away from commitment. She also needs to realize that there are other Mystics out there and she doesn't have to be alone. Like Phoebe (Lisa Kudrow) in *Friends* she can be herself regardless of what others think. She needs to find and express her free spirit.

What happened to her at an early age to make this archetype dominate her personality? Was she abused, pushing her into her own world? Did she see so much pain she opted out of ordinary life? Was she encouraged to be psychic? Was her mother interested in the paranormal?

To grow, this archetype is best paired with one of the following:

❍ The Gladiator—can teach her about feeling and expressing intense emotions.

❍ The Seducer or Seductive Muse—can teach her about sexuality and loosening up her shy, quiet nature.

❍ Messiah—can push her further into the spirit realms, giving her a chance to act out her convictions.

THE MYSTIC
Assets:
- Loves to be alone most of the time.
- Tries to keep the peace no matter the cost.
- Values her home life and solitude.

- Works carefully and slowly on one task at a time as if there's more than enough time.
- Is able to resist others who try to manipulate her.
- Takes part in a spiritual life.
- May be into the occult.
- Lives without material desires and expensive possessions.
- May be a vegetarian.
- Is into recycling and saving the earth.
- Doesn't care if others see her as eccentric or spacey.

Flaws:
- Doesn't know how to have fun with others.
- Lives in isolation even if others are around.
- Is shy and somewhat timid at times.
- Needs to learn assertiveness.
- Lives in her head too much.
- Doesn't really want to be "here" and may dream of other planets or dimensions.

The Villainous Side of the Mystic: The Betrayer

As a villain, the Mystic is the nice old lady who secretly poisons her husband. She can use her quiet nice nature to disguise her dark side so well no one would ever guess she was capable of doing anything wrong. Her sunny disposition can mask a monster lurking beneath the surface.

She's so unobtrusive people assume she's nothing more than a sweet shy person who could do no wrong. When people learn that she isn't what they expected they feel deeply betrayed. They set a higher standard for her than most women.

When she feels trapped by a family member she snaps and

tries to regain control of her life and home. Rejection can also make her lose control.

She has a tendency to avoid people and social situations. She's so afraid of doing something wrong that she tries to please everyone in all situations. This causes her so much stress she snaps. She feels inadequate and is terrified of rejection. She has no close relationships, is inhibited and socially inept, and is reluctant to take risks.

She thinks people never really look at her and never try to see the real woman inside. She happily gives them the "quiet little woman" stereotype to hide her deviant nature. If married she may feel her husband is a pain who takes away all her peace and quiet. She justifies her actions by saying she may kill someone but they won't feel a thing.

THE BETRAYER

- Usually feels trapped.
- Uses the "quiet little woman" stereotype to her advantage.
- Thinks of herself first and foremost.
- Has no problem taking a life or breaking a commandment because she goes to church and pays her dues.
- Relies on the kindness of strangers.
- Lets others feel good about helping her so they let their guard down.
- Is an expert liar.
- Maybe a sociopath. Very often a mental illness can be the cause of her deviant behavior.
- Is socially inept.
- Is afraid to take risks and make friends.
- Wants to be alone.
- Feels inadequate and fears rejection.

- Tries to please everyone around her and may snap under the pressure.

Hestia in Action
Mystic/Betrayer TV Heroes

Phoebe Buffay (Lisa Kudrow) in *Friends*

Dharma Freedom Finkelstein Montgomery (Jenna Elfman) in *Dharma & Greg*

Willow Rosenberg (Alyson Hannigan) in *Buffy the Vampire Slayer*

Mystic/Betrayer Film Heroes

Beverly Sutphin (Kathleen Turner) in *Serial Mom*

Marina (Demi Moore) in *The Butcher's Wife*

Annie Hall (Diane Keaton) in *Annie Hall*

Mystic/Betrayer Literary and Historical Heroes

Aunt Jet and Aunt Frances in *Practical Magic* by Alice Hoffman

Dolores Claiborne in *Dolores Claiborne* by Stephen King

Grandmother in *Flowers in the Attic* by V.C. Andrews

Julia in *Hideous Kinky* by Esther Freud

Eugenia Alabaster in *Angels and Insects* by A.S. Byatt

Beth March in *Little Women* by Louisa May Alcott

Muriel Pritchett in *The Accidental Tourist* by Anne Tyler

Blanche DuBois in *A Streetcar Named Desire* by Tennessee Williams

Chapter 9

Isis

The Female Messiah and the Destroyer

Surrounded by light, Isis walks across the earth bringing change, transformation and knowledge wherever she goes. She illuminates all she comes into contact with. She alone holds the words of life and death, for she alone knows the secret name of God. Those in her favor are blessed with the mysteries of eternal life, and those who wish to stay as they are fear her transforming presence. They will fight change with their last breath and will wish harm upon her, calling her unholy. Unconcerned with those of closed minds, she moves on with her mission to help her children find salvation and freedom. She is beauty, love, compassion and transformation.

The Female Messiah

The Messiah is the archetype of androgyny. Both the male and female version of this archetype are identical except for the fact that the male preaches and shows the way to love and enlightenment while the female is the way to love and enlightenment. This is probably why we hear so much more about male saints and yogis than female saints and yoginis.

The Female Messiah archetype can also contain any of the other archetypes, which will help her to achieve her goals in this lifetime. For example, Joan of Arc was a savior of her people who embodied the Artemis/Amazon archetype in battle.

The Female Messiah may not know of her connection to the Divine but just be "driven" to accomplish something important. In this respect she isn't working on a spiritual goal; it seems her whole life is for one purpose and that purpose

In Arthurian legend, the Lady of the Lake, a Female Messiah, presents Arthur with the famed sword Excalibur.

affects the lives of thousands of people.

The Female Messiah has the ability to see the whole picture when it comes to any problem. She never jumps to conclusions or gets involved in the gossip or drama of everyday life. She's a detached observer who sees all sides and understands all views.

She respects all religions and belief systems. She gives freely of herself because she knows what she puts out comes back to her threefold.

The Female Messiah isn't as easily accepted by the masses as a spiritual authority figure because of her gender. If she remains somewhat quiet and allows others to speak of her for a time, she'll later have the opportunity to speak out about her views. It's OK for her to have a message that's about the feminine traits of love and compassion, but her message may be much harsher than that, as was Joan of Arc's. This can cause trouble for her unless women are viewed as equals. She can be thought of as hysterical or may be pushed aside and called "just a housewife" to demean her and her accomplishments.

She may not realize her Divine connections but be born with a strong pull toward a goal and a willingness to sacrifice herself for it. Think of what the women who fought for the right to vote sacrificed, or the chance Rosa Parks took when she refused to give up her seat.

What Does the Female Messiah Care About?

✪ The Female Messiah understands the plight of women and the feminine in a patriarchal society, and she cares about elevating the female status.

✪ She cares about herself as well as others. Every living thing is a manifestation of the Divine to her.

✪ She cares about others recognizing their own divine nature. She wants everyone to grow spiritually.

✪ She pays special attention to the children and animals because they can't help themselves.

✪ She values healing the soul above healing the body. She can't take away the pain of another who needs to learn from his experience even though she may be a gifted healer.

What Does the Female Messiah Fear?

✪ The Female Messiah fears people will be led astray by those on the wrong path or by their own desire to please.

✪ She fears she'll be persecuted but embraces it as part of her destiny. She sees the greater good of every event and only suffers if her family is persecuted because of her actions.

✪ She fears she'll run out of time to fulfill her mission or that she'll have to watch others suffer.

What Motivates the Female Messiah?

✪ The aesthetic need to be connected to something greater than herself motivates her as well as her desire to give and receive unconditional love.

✪ She knows she must battle her demons to maintain her connection to the divine. She has moments of clarity and bliss but then she must learn to integrate this experience with the tasks of everyday life. She doesn't place herself above anyone else.

✪ Her sense of purpose is so strong she can do nothing else but be motivated to reach her goal.

How Do Other Characters See the Female Messiah?

✪ Others see her as either good or bad; there's no in-between for her. They view her as idealistic, crazy and on a power trip, or as divine, wise and giving. It makes no difference to her.

✪ Many people are jealous of her connection with the Divine, especially clergy. Think of Joan of Arc; her connection to God through her voices led her to be burned at the stake.

Developing the Character Arc

This archetype doesn't necessarily change in her character arc but instead grows stronger through her fears.

Lady Godiva sacrificed her modesty and volunteered to ride naked through the town in order to get her husband to lower the townspeople's taxes. Her selflessness is a trait of the female Messiah archetype.

Look at your character's main goal in the story and then at the fears you've selected to use against her. What can help her overcome her fear? Does she need to learn how to be centered in a crowd of angry people? Does she need to find her identity as an individual separate from the group? Does she need to learn to stand up for her beliefs?

Very often the Messiah needs to learn to let go of the outcome of events and to trust the spirit who guides her. She needs to stick to her own guns and fully believe in herself no matter what the outcome.

She needs to face her accusers and her own doubts. If she is highly psychic and sensitive she may wonder about her sanity. Others' opinions of her can cause her great distress when she's first taking a stand.

When did her goal or view become strong in her life and why? Was she baptized? Did she go through a right of passage? Were her parents activists? Were they spiritual or religious people? Was she sensitive or psychic as a child? Did she see harm or kindness done to others?

Most likely this archetype will help other characters to grow instead of growing herself.

⊘ She may find laughter with the Maiden.

⊘ And nice silence with the Mystic.

⊘ The Protector can be a protective ally for her.

⊘ And the Warlock can be a bit of a challenge.

The Female Messiah

Assets:

- Cares more for others than herself.
- Has a healthy sense of who she is.
- Has a strong spiritual belief system to pull her through tough times.
- Seemed smarter and older than most adults when she was a child.
- Is willing to sacrifice herself for the good of all.
- Stands up for her beliefs no matter the cost.
- Renounces material possessions.
- Lives in tune with nature.
- Has an inner strength that never dies.

Flaws:

- Tells people the truth even if it's harsh.
- Pushes people beyond their limits to help them grow.
- Doubts herself.

The Villainous Side of the Female Messiah: The Destroyer

The Female Messiah isn't really a villain in the sense of only being concerned with her own gain and desires. She's a villain in the sense of protecting the highest good for all. As the destroyer she'll drop the atom bomb to stop Hitler—the end is positive but the means are destructive and harsh. She's the mother who says, "I brought you into this world, and I can take you out if you don't behave."

She does this for your own good and not hers. She'll kill one to save many but who's to say if that one will be your child or not? She seems almost without emotion as she makes such decisions. She'll let you die from a disease she can cure if it'll help your spiritual growth.

There's no emotional or mental involvement in what she does. It's as if she's programmed by the Divine to take care of things. She's like a robot given a mission to accomplish—she just does it.

She doesn't care to justify herself to others; they'll never fully understand her power or the burden she carries. She believes everyone has karma to work out. Do unto others or she'll help others do unto you in order to teach you a lesson.

THE DESTROYER
- Sees things in black and white.
- Is unemotional about hurting one to save many. She sees the spirit not the flesh.
- Feels the pain of transformation is necessary.
- Loves to challenge people and push their limits.
- Is a harsh wielder of justice.
- Punishes for the greater good of all.
- Knows some things can't be explained.
- Won't try to reassure others or play favorites.

Isis in Action
Messiah/Destroyer TV Heroes
Monica (Roma Downey) in *Touched By an Angel*

Messiah/Destroyer Film Heroes
Bernadette Soubirous (Jennifer Jones) in *The Song of Bernadette*

Leeloo (Milla Jovovich) in *The Fifth Element*

Mary of Nazareth (Pernilla August) in *Mary, Mother of Jesus*

Trinity (Carrie-Anne Moss) in *The Matrix*

Jade Fox (Pei-pei Cheng) in *Crouching Tiger, Hidden Dragon*

Norma Rae (Sally Field) in *Norma Rae*

Erin Brockovich (Julia Roberts) in *Erin Brockovich*

Messiah/Destroyer Literary and Historical Heroes
Joan of Arc

Wonder Woman

Lady of the Lake in Arthurian Legend

Lady Godiva

Morgaine in *The Mists of Avalon* by Marion Zimmer Bradley

Mary Magdalene in *The Moon Under Her Feet* by Clysta Kinstler

Angela McCourt in *Angela's Ashes* by Frank McCourt

Hester Prynne in *The Scarlet Letter* by Nathaniel Hawthorne

Galadriel in *The Lord of the Rings* by J.R.R. Tolkien

Chapter 10

Persephone
The Maiden and the Troubled Teen

Dancing through the fields, Persephone picks flowers as the sun sets. Without a care in the world, she stops to watch butterflies flutter around her feet. In the distance she sees a magnificent narcissus flower and runs toward it. Picking the flower, her mind so absorbed in the moment, she doesn't see Hades rising up from the Earth to kidnap her as his bride, the flower his bait. The harsh reality of life has taken her by surprise and awakened her from her blissful stupor. She learns to use her suffering to help others by guiding the souls of the dead to their final resting places. Her mother's grief at her absence allows her to return above ground in the spring when the flowers bloom.

The Maiden

The Maiden lives a charmed playful life unconcerned with annoying daily errands and problems. "It's no big deal" is her mantra. She's not stressed out because she never worries about things. She takes risks because she feels invulnerable and pushes others to follow her on her exploits like Lucy does with Ethel in *I Love Lucy*. Her self-confidence rubs off on others.

Age isn't a factor when creating this archetype since she may be in her forties yet still acts like a little girl who wants to party and have fun. Her youthful looks never fade. She hasn't grown up and doesn't want to. Marriage, kids and responsibility aren't foremost on her mind.

When something happens that pushes her to open her eyes she'll find that she has a big heart and a great capacity to be a healer and a guide for others.

In *Tess of the d'Urbervilles* by Thomas Hardy, both Angel Clare (an Artist) and Alec d'Urberville (a Seducer) idealize Tess (a Maiden) as a young and pure innocent.

The Maiden doesn't realize the danger that lurks in the world. Trauma can be a rite of passage for her, opening her eyes to reality. There are occasions where she may suppress a traumatic experience as if it never happened, but she then becomes a ticking time bomb as similar situations in her life force the memory to the surface.

In *Daisy Miller* by Henry James, the title character shares traits with the Maiden archetype; her youthful naiveté eventually leads to her death.

What Does the Maiden Care About?

✪ The Maiden cares about her relationship with her mother. She tries to stay on the good side of others who support and take of her. She'll hold her tongue and keep her opinions to herself to keep the peace.

✪ She likes being dependent upon others; it removes responsibility for her life from her own shoulders. She prefers to let others worry about paying the bills.

✪ She loves to meet new people and have fun. She's always looking for the next fad, trend or game to play. Everything new and different catches her eye. She's never bored. She likes to take classes because they only last a few weeks and change often. She can meet new people every semester.

What Does the Maiden Fear?

✪ The Maiden fears having to make decisions for herself. She'll bother everyone around her until someone makes a decision for her. She doesn't want to fend for herself if she doesn't have to. She believes there's power in making others do things for you.

✪ She doesn't want others to pass her by and grow up without her. She needs people to play with.

✪ Her greatest fear is being trapped in a nine-to-five job or a controlling relationship with a man. She needs her space and freedom. Her spirit is fragile.

✪ People think she's naive, and she fears being attacked. She's not totally immune to the world around her; she tries to enjoy life in spite of it.

What Motivates the Maiden?

✪ Safety and security is what motivates the Maiden. She needs to know that there's someone there to catch her if she falls. Whether she has faced the harshness in life or not, or if she is rich or poor, she knows she needs someone to support her free lifestyle.

✪ If she ever faces a traumatic situation her need for security and protection will grow.

✪ Freedom to be herself is the most valued thing in her life. She has to express herself and her desires, but at the same time she has to please others enough so they don't write her out of the will, so to speak.

✪ She enjoys being different, special, talked about. She loves to do outrageous things. She loves Lucy Ricardo.

How Do Other Characters See the Maiden?

✪ Women see her as young, inexperienced and aloof. Men see her as sexy and childlike, a woman they can control and

In Arthurian legend, the chivalrous Lancelot rescues his love Guinevere (a Maiden) from the evil knight Meligrance. (The abduction of Guinevere mirrors Persephone's abduction by Hades in Greek mythology.)

rescue. She seems to attract dominating men.

○ A lot of men say they're attracted to her innocence and want to take care of her, but they can become overprotective and bossy. They just like her because she makes them feel young.

○ She wears girlish clothing sometimes, and alluring and sexy clothing other times.

Developing the Character Arc

Look at your character's main goal in the story and then at the fears you've selected to use against her. What can she learn to help her overcome her fear? Does she need to learn how to take care of herself? Does she need to find her spiritual side? Does she need to transcend her desire to be around people and at parties all the time?

Very often the Maiden needs to be forced to stand on her own two feet. She needs to support herself and make commitments. She needs to gain faith in her abilities and see strength in her character. She needs to be aware of the harshness of life and take off her rose-colored glasses.

She can be a very strong person who gives openly to others, guiding them through pain and hardships. She needs to see this gift she has within herself. She is very innocent and pure at heart if she'll only turn her gaze inward and see herself for who she really is.

What happened to her at an early age to make this archetype dominate her personality? Was she spoiled? Did her parents hide all problems and pain from her? Did an older sibling do everything for her? Did she have a learning disorder and was treated as special?

To grow, this archetype is best paired with one of the following:

○ **The Woman's Man**—can show her the strength that lies

Little Red Riding Hood is an example of the Maiden archetype—her eyes are closed to the dangers of the Big Bad Wolf.

inside her and can help her understand and accept her sensitivities and spiritual gifts.

✪ **The Warlock—**would abduct her in some way, waking

her up and taking her out of the protected little world she has made for herself.

○ **The Amazon**—would teach her how to care for herself and to be strong. She can show her how to accept her own power and sensitivity as a positive thing. She can also drag her out of her protected world.

○ **The Overcontrolling Mother**—can be so overbearing and controlling that she pushes the Maiden out of the house where she then learns to fend for herself.

The Maiden

Assets:

- Loves to play and go to parties.
- Is close to her mother or otherwise distraught if she isn't.
- Switches friends and interests often; she loves variety.
- Doesn't have plans for her future beyond Saturday night.
- Seems very innocent and gentle.
- Can be a wonderful listener.
- Can help people through trauma.
- Can be sensitive and psychic.

Flaws:

- Depends on someone else for her survival and freedom.
- Needs attention and loves the spotlight.
- Has trouble committing to one relationship.
- May not understand the consequences of her actions.
- Walks around with rose-colored glasses as if nothing will happen to her.
- Keeps her opinions to herself to please others.

The Villainous Side of the Maiden: The Troubled Teen

As a villain, the Maiden is the out-of-control teen obsessed with fun, parties, drugs, sex—everything in excess. Grades and rules don't matter because she doesn't care about the future.

She may commit a crime not understanding the consequences of her actions. She may be talked into sex to please a boy and get pregnant because of her ignorance of birth control. When these things happen she expects her parents or family members to pitch in and help her. In her eyes they better be there to pay for lawyers, watch the baby or whatever else she needs. She's never taken responsibility for her actions before, and she won't start taking them now.

She's passive/aggressive, saying she'll take control of her life but doing everything but. When family members and friends aren't there for her she'll do whatever it takes to get them to help her, even attempt suicide to get their attention. Everyone else's life must stop to deal with her antics. Anyone who cares about her will never get a decent night's sleep. Jaded, depressed and disillusioned with the world, the Troubled Teen often ends up in front of a judge, the courts forced to set her straight. Most of the time childhood abuse is what fuels her anger.

She has a pattern of irresponsible behavior that lacks morals and ethics. She shows a lack of responsibility for herself and uses superficial charm to manipulate others.

She is self-centered when it comes to her problems. "No one else matters but me" is her mantra. She believes she's special and above the law. She feels entitled to be around others she views as unique and special. She can be arrogant and lacks empathy toward others. She often fantasizes about how successful she'll become because she deserves it.

She feels like no one told her this world was so horrible and she didn't ask to be born. She wishes everyone would just leave her alone. She believes it's her body and she'll do whatever she wants with it. She doesn't have time to worry about tomorrow because it may never come. When she dies she wants to look back on a life full of friends and fun.

THE TROUBLED TEEN

- Hates rules and all types of authority. She's anti-establishment.
- Is depressed, angry and selfish.
- Steals and fights.
- Has a death wish and takes a lot of risks.
- Is vulnerable to cults and resistance groups.
- Uses superficial charm to manipulate others.
- Is loyal to fellow criminals.
- Likes to hurt her family because they hurt her.
- Can't love or care for other living things.
- Has buried her true self.
- Feels entitled and special, above the law.
- Fantasizes about her own future success.
- Is irresponsible.

Persephone in Action
Maiden/Troubled Teen TV Heroes

Cordelia Chase (Charisma Carpenter) in *Buffy the Vampire Slayer* and *Angel*

Lucy Ricardo (Lucille Ball) in *I Love Lucy*

Phoebe Halliwell (Alyssa Milano) in *Charmed*

Rachel Green (Jennifer Aniston) in *Friends*

Maiden/Troubled Teen Film Heroes

Cher Horowitz (Alicia Silverstone) in *Clueless*
Mary Jensen Matthews (Cameron Diaz) in *There's Something About Mary*
Louise Dickinson (Geena Davis) in *Thelma & Louise*
Mia Wallace (Uma Thurman) in *Pulp Fiction*
Sandra Dee (Olivia Newton-John) in *Grease*
Jen Yu (Ziyi Zhang) in *Crouching Tiger, Hidden Dragon*

Maiden/Troubled Teen Literary and Historical Heroes

Antigone
Guinevere in Arthurian Legend
Little Red Riding Hood
Princess in *Sleeping Beauty*
Alice in *Alice in Wonderland* by Lewis Carroll
Dorothy in *The Wizard of Oz* by L. Frank Baum
Dolores "Lolita" Haze in *Lolita* by Vladimir Nabokov
Margaret in *Are You There God? It's Me, Margaret* by Judy Blume
Juliet in *Romeo and Juliet* by William Shakespeare
Ophelia in *Hamlet* by William Shakespeare
Emma in *Emma* by Jane Austen
Daisy Miller in *Daisy Miller* by Henry James
Daisy Buchanan in *The Great Gatsby* by F. Scott Fitzgerald
Beloved in *Beloved* by Toni Morrison
Tess in *Tess of the d'Urbervilles* by Thomas Hardy

III Creating Male Heroes and Villains

Chapter 11

Apollo
The Businessman and the Traitor

Underneath the brilliant shining Sun, strides the god Apollo along the beach. He surveys the ocean, preferring to look at the horizon instead of examining what lies beneath the waves. His mind is always set on events in the far distance. He carries with him a bow and arrows, which allow him to attack from a comforting distance. He glides through the night watching over innocent young children and seeking out a challenger to polish his skill as an expert archer. His logical mind makes him the dispenser of justice, and his strong willpower allows him to accomplish any goal he sets for himself.

The Businessman

The Businessman is a man on the go who constantly thinks about his work. His strong logical mind makes him great at being a team player and a trustworthy employee but doesn't help him to be a great husband or father. He doesn't know how to let loose and play with the kids, so he often takes work home to avoid family life.

It's hard for him to go on vacation and have a good time with his family. Intimacy and sitting still for extended periods of time seem like a waste of time and effort to him. He'll often invite business associates and their families to come along on such vacations to kill two birds with one stone.

He understands the nature of cause and effect and lives his life accordingly. He can set goals and reach them where other men fail. His focus is rock solid; his actions clear and precise. He loves to plan and set high standards for himself and others, but he often falls short of his ultimate goals because

When the title character in Nathaniel Hawthorne's story "Young Goodman Brown" encounters a chaotic world of sin in the forest, his Businessman reliance on order is put to the test.

he lacks the ruthlessness to reach them. He does well in a large corporation or on the faculty of a large college.

What Does the Businessman Care About?

⊘ The Businessman cares about his career. He's able to plan his career path and focus on his goals. Every project he undertakes and every contact he makes is done so with the knowledge of how it'll further his career. He doesn't waste time or effort and can't understand other men who don't share his enthusiasm.

⊘ He enjoys being the calm and centered man in the room

Spock's logical thinking skills and calm demeanor are characteristics of the Businessman archetype.

to settle arguments and bring about order and peace. He would make a great judge because he also prefers not to fight or to get physically involved in sticky situations.

✪ He enjoys strategic planning and wants to be a part of a team.

✪ Competition is fun to him, with either men or women. He respects others who are after the same promotion he is. They're planners just like him.

In *A Christmas Carol*, by Charles Dickens, Jacob Marley's ghost tries to warn Ebenezer Scrooge about his miserly insistence on rules and order. These are traits of the villainous side of the Businessman—the Traitor.

What Does the Businessman Fear?

✪ He fears losing his career and having to get a job. He loves what he does for a living; it's his identity and whole reason for being.

✪ His emotions and any type of intimacy are foreign to him. He may have several girlfriends at once because he fears getting too close to any of them. They have to understand and support his workaholic lifestyle.

✪ Chaos is his enemy; he isn't equipped to handle anything spontaneous or random. He must know where things fit and why. He's always thinking logically and striving for order in his life just as he strives for it in his work.

✪ Rejection isn't something he handles very well especially if it comes from a woman.

What Motivates the Businessman?

✪ His biggest motivators are self-esteem and self-respect. He wants to be looked up to and recognized for his efforts, but at the same time he's not looking to stand apart from the team. He would never want to be the sole responsible person for the company.

✪ Competition can goad him into trying new things. Any chance to use his mental skills always grabs his attention.

✪ Success is another motivator. He'll do anything to move up the corporate ladder.

How Do Other Characters See the Businessman?

✪ Some see him as phony as he seems to talk to only those who can help his company or further his career. He doesn't care what they think. Success is more important than friendships. Friendships won't pay for his retirement.

✪ He's a sharp dresser but not much more than his fellow workers. Sometimes he'll wear a colorful tie that stands out, but that's as far as he'll go in being different. He wants to project the right image.

✪ He has no passion or love for life and seems devoid of compassion at times. No one knows what he's thinking behind his solid eyes.

In mystery stories, detectives display Businessman characteristics, such as a reliance on logic and a need for order.

Developing the Character Arc

Look at your character's main goal in the story and then at the fears you've selected to use against him. What does he need to learn to help him overcome his fear? Does he need to learn how to be alone and happy with it? Does he need to connect emotionally with his family? Did his wife die and he needs to care for the kids? Did he get passed over for a promotion and his career is failing?

Very often the Businessman needs to learn how to let go of his inhibitions and goals. He needs to learn humility and compassion for others. He needs to get in touch with his emotions and find the ability to relate to others as a person and not a figurehead.

What happened to him at an early age to make this archetype dominate his personality? Did his parents make him do well in school, pushing him to succeed? Did he see his father humiliated? Did his parents lose everything because they weren't focused and dedicated to their jobs? Was he picked on for being uncoordinated and now overcompensates with mental ability?

To grow, this archetype is best paired with one of the following:

♥ **The Artist**—can teach him to get in touch with the feminine qualities of love and emotions.

♥ **The Seducer**—can teach him how to let go of the consequences of his actions and have some fun in life.

♥ **The Mystic**—can teach him how to be a spiritual person and how to be by himself without a lot of work and activities to numb his mind. This quiet time may bring up memories and feelings that he is trying to suppress through his workaholic lifestyle.

♥ **The Gorgon**—can humiliate him and teach him to be humble. She can turn his life upside down causing chaos and uncertainty.

THE BUSINESSMAN

Assets:

- Likes blending into the team at work.
- Is concerned about his image at work and is a neat dresser.
- Has a strong will to get things done.
- Is a logical and strategic thinker and can be a great analyst, detective and teacher.
- Thrives on order.
- Finds work and new ideas to be his only passions.
- Can be loyal and trustworthy.
- Loves to help others when he can use his expertise.

Flaws:

- Obsesses about his career.
- Gives his attention only to those who can further his career.
- Has trouble expressing his emotions.
- Can be arrogant.
- Identifies with the aggressor when attacked and perpetuates the cycle of violence.
- Doesn't handle rejection well.
- Lacks spontaneity, hates chaos and is inflexible.

The Villainous Side of the Businessman: The Traitor

As a villain the Businessman is the Traitor. Work comes first to this man. If he sees his company facing disaster he'll go to extreme lengths to cover up any wrongdoing. He'll tell on his co-workers if they do something that threatens the company, even if the company is doing harm. His mental expertise bestows trust on him; many don't have a choice but to trust him because they don't have the knowledge to dispute him. This puts others at his mercy. When things go wrong he feels he's the one to dispense justice, and he does it with a cool but unfeeling demeanor. He can be without mercy because he's been lost for so long inside his head and away from his feelings.

When things get chaotic his emotions fly out of control making him do things he never thought he could. His logical mind holds his emotions at bay, but when situations defy logic his mind is pushed to a breaking point.

He uses rules and order to avoid his feelings. He's a perfectionist with a strong preoccupation for details, rules, lists, order and schedules, which interfere with him actually completing a task. He can't throw anything away. He has trouble letting other people help him with his work unless they submit to his way of doing things. He wants everything to be just so, and when others don't comply he snaps. He's like Howard Payne (Dennis Hopper) in the movie *Speed* who plays with Officer Jack Craven (Keanu Reeves) by making him solve puzzles to get to the next clue. He loves to show off his inventions and expertise.

While it's true that most villains don't believe they're bad, this villain truly believes he's the good guy. Others are at fault; they caused the chaos, and he deserves better than that. He wants to show how valuable he is and will prove that they can't get by without him. He'll sell his inventions to the highest bidder because he feels he should get paid for his work.

THE TRAITOR

- Feels undervalued.
- Wants respect and recognition for his efforts.
- Doesn't have any loyalty once he feels abandoned by the group.
- Will do whatever it takes to bring order back into his life.
- Wants to teach others a lesson and doesn't feel he's a villain at all.
- Can't sit still and accept rejection.
- Betrays only those he feels betrayed him.
- Is obsessive in his need to organize and work out his plan of attack.
- Views people as pawns in a game of chess.
- Likes long drawn-out attacks that challenge him as well as his opponent. He may even befriend his rivals.

Apollo in Action

Businessman/Traitor TV Heroes

Dr. Frasier Crane (Kelsey Grammer) and Dr. Niles Crane (David Hyde Pierce) in *Frasier*

Lieutenant Columbo (Peter Falk) in *Columbo*

Roy "The Professor" Hinkley Jr. (Russell Johnson) in *Gilligan's Island*

Commander Spock (Leonard Nimoy) in *Star Trek*

Richard Fish (Greg Germann) in *Ally McBeal*

Alex P. Keaton (Michael J. Fox) in *Family Ties*

Businessman/Traitor Film Heroes

David Levinson (Jeff Goldblum) in *Independence Day*

Dr. Egon Spengler (Harold Ramis) in *Ghostbusters*

Gordon Gekko (Michael Douglas) in *Wall Street*

Howard Payne (Dennis Hopper) in *Speed*

Jerry Maguire (Tom Cruise) in *Jerry Maguire*

Professor Henry Higgins (Rex Harrison) in *My Fair Lady*

Edward Lewis (Richard Gere) in *Pretty Woman*

Alvy Singer (Woody Allen) in *Annie Hall*

Businessman/Traitor Literary and Historical Heroes

Dr. Alan Grant in *Jurassic Park* by Michael Crichton

Sherlock Holmes in stories by Sir Arthur Conan Doyle

Young Goodman Brown in "Young Goodman Brown" by Nathaniel Hawthorne

Hercule Poirot in novels by Agatha Christie

Ebenezer Scrooge in *A Christmas Carol* by Charles Dickens

Willy Loman in *Death of a Salesman* by Arthur Miller

Mr. Darcy in *Pride and Prejudice* by Jane Austen

Macon Leary in *The Accidental Tourist* by Anne Tyler

George Babbitt in *Babbitt* by Sinclair Lewis

Joseph K. in *The Trial* by Franz Kafka

Chapter 12

Ares
The Protector and the Gladiator

High on the hill overlooking the battlefield, all of the gods watch the war taking place below except for Ares. In full armor, he delightfully joins in the fight. He fights to satiate his lust for blood rather than to win a noble cause. Everything physical is joyous to him, and his passion leaves all in his wake breathless. He is known as the protector of the community and of families, but any reason to join in a brawl is a good enough reason for him.

The Protector

The Protector is a man who lives in his body instead of his head. He feels everything intensely and craves physical activity of all kinds. He protects the ones he loves so fiercely it seems as if he's fighting for his own pleasure alone. He doesn't need much of a reason to fight or react harshly in a situation.

He lives on eggshells, as if everyone were out to get him. He's like a ticking time bomb just waiting to go off. At the same time he can be fiercely loyal and protective, making women feel special and cared for. His sensual nature and bodily expertise make him a great lover. A strong need for spontaneity and risks will drive him in and out of people's lives, making him not someone to commit to.

Career goals aren't foremost in his mind; the future seems far away. His life is full of adventure and risks, and he likes it that way.

An example of the Gladiator archetype, Sonny Corleone (James Caan, third from left) in *The Godfather* has an impulsive, aggressive nature and is fiercely protective of his family.

What Does the Protector Care About?

❂ The Protector loves to get physical. His body is everything to him; it's how he experiences life. Dancing, singing, laughing and fighting—that's him.

❂ He cares about winning the fight whether it's on the football field or in the boardroom, though he's not really the corporate type.

❂ He cares about his friends and family and will jump at any chance to defend them without worrying about the consequences. Every attack on his family and friends is seen as an attack on him. He may channel this intensity to protect others into a charitable cause and can be a great activist. He shines when it comes to battling for others' rights.

❂ Travel and spontaneous women are his favorite pastimes.

What Does the Protector Fear?

✪ There's nothing another person can do to him that would make him feel fear. He fears only losing touch with his body and his abilities. To be sick or paralyzed is the same as death to him. He feels everything intensely.

✪ He fears not being able to protect those he cares about.

✪ He would hate a job where he had to sit at a desk all day, and he doesn't understand men who do. He'd rather take a cut in pay to be a construction worker; at least there's some risk involved.

✪ He hates having to use his mind too much. He prefers to jump to the physical solution to every problem that arises.

What Motivates the Protector?

✪ His biggest motivator is survival. Every attack, small or large, is a threat to his survival. He lives each day on the edge. Any small threat can be the beginning of a larger one, and he'll nip it in the bud. Many harsh words people speak are just that—words—but he takes them very seriously. "Kill or be killed" is his motto. So is "an eye for an eye."

✪ Life without risk is boring to him. If he's not protecting and defending then he's searching for the next big challenge. He's the first one into the water and loves to make others feel silly for being afraid to follow him. He leads people to take risks with him and enjoy life.

How Do Other Characters See the Protector?

✪ He's seen as either intense and passionate or thick-headed and bullish. He lives in the moment and reacts without thinking. He doesn't care much about what others think because he is enjoying himself.

✪ He wants others to sense the dark need for battle that

lurks behind his eyes. He wants to intimidate.

○ His clothes are always practical for the situation he's in. He needs to be free to move around and join in so he won't dress in a suit, no matter the event he's attending.

Developing the Character Arc

Look at your character's main goal in the story and then at the fears you've selected to use against him. What does he need to learn to help him overcome his fear? Does he need to learn to use his mind instead of his body? Does he need to learn how to sit still and be alone? Does he need to temper his need to take risks? Does he need to learn how to control his temper? Does he need to get a steady-paying job or career?

Very often the Protector needs to learn self-control. He's always flying off the handle and needs to learn to take a deep breath, step back and assess the situation before reacting. He needs to learn how to defend himself with words instead of fists.

What happened to him at an early age to make this archetype dominate his personality? Was his father abusive? Did his mother dance around the house a lot and play games with him? Was he picked on as a kid and then swear he'd be strong? Did he see his father get hurt? Were his parents activists who taught him about fighting for causes? Was his mother hurt and he couldn't help her?

To grow, this archetype is best paired with one of the following:

○ **The King**—can teach him self-control and discipline of his actions.

○ **The Troubled Teen**—may not want to be rescued, so the Protector will have to learn to let go of someone who doesn't want his help.

○ **The Father's Daughter**—is great at using her logical mind

Romeo's quick nature leads him to fall in love with Juliet (a Maiden) the first time he sees her. His impetuous nature and bold wooing of Juliet is characteristic of the Protector archetype.

and can teach him how to fight with words. Her influence can calm him down and force him to reflect before he acts out.

 ۞ The Overcontrolling Mother—will teach him to be disciplined with her controlling nature. Her emotions and rage can easily match his own; she's a worthy opponent. He can't lash out at her physically without paying a high price.

THE PROTECTOR
Assets:
- Is very physical as opposed to mental.
- Forgoes career success for fun and travel.
- Will fight to save those he loves, never giving up.

- Will fight for a good cause when others are afraid to stand up.
- Loves to sing, dance and make love.
- Searches for the next big thrill, challenge or risk.

Flaws:

- Physically reacts to an attack without thinking.
- Acts as if he's fighting for his survival all the time.
- Lives on the edge.
- Has trouble considering the consequences of his actions.
- Is merciless in his actions and believes in an eye for an eye.

The Villainous Side of the Protector: The Gladiator

As a villain the Protector turns into the Gladiator. He's not out to protect or save the ones he loves or to fight for a good cause. Instead he's out for the lust of battle and blood. He fights and destroys for the sheer pleasure and power it brings. He lusts after the roar of the crowd, which he may get from seeing himself in the news.

His lust for risk taking makes him put other people's lives in danger, and he doesn't give it a second thought. He's the man who drives twice the speed limit just to beat his friend home and doesn't think about the safety of other drivers on the road. Life is a game to him.

He has ingrained, maladaptive patterns of behavior with impulsive and unpredictable actions. He has frequent inappropriate temper outbursts and an unstable self-image. He takes no responsibility for his actions and often plays the victim when confronted about his behavior.

Stress-related anxiety plagues him as do feelings of real or imagined abandonment. He always feels empty inside and tries to compensate by taking risks that put himself and others in danger. Danger is all that can make him feel. He can't stand being alone and may drive others crazy needing to always go out and find something to do.

He loves to fight and enjoys challenges and risks; it makes him feel alive. Life is so boring and cruel to him, and he won't be the one to suffer. Why should he care about killing someone else when he so readily accepts his own mortality? At least he'll go out with the roar of the crowd—a hero till the end. He isn't concerned with growing old because he doesn't expect to live long.

THE GLADIATOR

- Feels abandoned.
- Lusts after the roar of the crowd.
- Craves blood, death and battle.
- Is out of touch with his caring emotions; only feels rage and anger.
- Has frequent temper outbursts.
- Has a poor self-image.
- Can't stand to be alone.
- Wants to feel, and danger is all that he can feel.
- Takes risks to compensate for feeling so empty inside.
- Pushes others to take risks with him.
- Puts innocent people in danger.
- Plays the victim when confronted about his behavior.
- Doesn't expect to live long.
- Welcomes a valiant death.

Ares in Action

Protector/Gladiator TV Heroes

Lieutenant Worf (Michael Dorn) in *Star Trek: The Next Generation*

Detective Danny Sorenson (Rick Schroeder) in *NYPD Blue*

Detective Sergeant Rick Hunter (Fred Dryer) in *Hunter*

Michael Knight (David Hasselhoff) in *Knight Rider*

Sonny Crockett (Don Johnson) in *Miami Vice*

Protector/Gladiator Film Heroes

Rocky Balboa (Sylvester Stallone) in *Rocky*

Detective John McClane (Bruce Willis) in *Die Hard*

Archie Gates (George Clooney) in *Three Kings*

Cal Trask (James Dean) in *East of Eden*

Lieutenant Pete "Maverick" Mitchell (Tom Cruise) in *Top Gun*

Jack Colton (Michael Douglas) in *Romancing the Stone*

Han Solo (Harrison Ford) in *Star Wars*

"Sonny" Corleone (James Caan) in *The Godfather*

Protector/Gladiator Literary and Historical Heroes

Little John

Superman

Zorro

Lancelot

The Incredible Hulk

Thor

Romeo in *Romeo and Juliet* by William Shakespeare

Jack in *Lord of the Flies* by William Golding

Richard in *Rogue Warrior* series by Richard Marcinko

Chapter 13

Hades
The Recluse and the Warlock

Dwelling in the dark underworld, unable to find light, Hades lives inside his head. He has no need for friends or acquaintances but instead prefers to linger alone. His life is full of the richness of the imagination as he goes about his daily activities. His mind is always somewhere else. He never realized what he was missing in his life until he came upon the beautiful goddess Persephone. Seeing her he knew he needed some companionship to get through his life, but unschooled in the ways of love he kidnaps her and drags her into his underworld life. He steals her innocence and realizes how unfeeling he has become. As his love grows he decides to sacrifice part of his time with her so that she may visit her mother in the Spring. She has taught him compassion and self-awareness.

The Recluse

The Recluse is a man who has a rich inner life and creative spirit but can sometimes get lost in his own fantasies. He may be a sensitive man who can see other realms, a sort of psychic, and is in danger of totally withdrawing from reality altogether.

He can also be a great philosopher who spends hours reading and analyzing ideas. If he finds the right woman he can have a small family life and enjoy some companionship but the entire relationship is up to her. He has no skill in that department and may be distant for days at a time. Hestia is the perfect woman for him. She enjoys being alone.

When Hamlet (a Recluse) sees his father's ghost, he is forced out of his solitary world by a need for revenge. He later exhibits Warlock qualities, as he turns away Ophelia and seeks to bring about Claudius's downfall.

What Does the Recluse Care About?

⊙ The Recluse cares about being alone. He has a rich inner life and enjoys being inside his head. He's not comfortable around people, especially large groups, and would prefer to be a mountain man than a businessman. If he lives closer to the city he may opt to become a monk.

⊙ He cares only about his inner world; everyone else can keep their dramas to themselves. He doesn't want to be bothered by others at all. He likes being invisible in large groups.

⊙ He feels alien to everyone else and may want to move on to the next world, welcoming death.

⊙ He cares about his hobbies and projects, often spending hours and hours on one small task. He chooses to do every-

Many of the characters in Edgar Allan Poe's short stories, such as Roderick Usher in "The Fall of the House of Usher," demonstrate a solitary nature that is typical of the Recluse archetype.

thing himself rather than running down to the store to buy a gadget that may do the job.

What Does the Recluse Fear?

✪ The Recluse fears large groups of people. He loves his solitude, but a part of him may long for a small family unit to bring him some companionship.

✪ He fears losing his mind in one of his rich fantasy worlds, especially if he's highly psychic and can hear spirits.

✪ He's afraid of his own emotions and seems very bland, without personality at times.

✪ He fears the world will come upon him and swallow him up. He's afraid of people forcing themselves into his life.

With their solitary ramblings in the wilderness, many early explorers, such as Daniel Boone, exemplify the Recluse archetype.

His home base is the most important thing to him; it's his safety net.

What Motivates the Recluse?

✪ The Recluse's biggest motivator is the need to know and understand. He lives in his head and is always thinking and analyzing. He uses his need to understand his world to occupy his time. He is a great philosopher who can spend ages questioning the mysteries of life.

✪ His need to be alone motivates him to do whatever it takes to find a place where he can be alone.

✪ At some point severe loneliness may cause him to seek out a mate or find a friend.

How Do Other Characters See the Recluse?

❂ Others may see him as a bland person devoid of personality. They wonder if he's insane at times because he obsesses about the deeper meaning of things.

❂ He pays no attention to the clothes he wears or the food he eats. He's too much in his head. He's somewhat like Albert Einstein who wore the same type of suit every day.

❂ He seems fragmented and disorderly, always looking for things he's misplaced.

Developing the Character Arc

Look at your character's main goal in the story and then at the fears you've selected to use against him. What does he need to learn to help him overcome his fear? Does he need to learn to speak in front of large groups? Does he need to organize his life? Does he need to learn how to feel and express love? Does he have to interact with a large group of people in order to save his home?

Very often the Recluse needs to learn how to relate to people. He needs to learn that human companionship has its own rewards and can enrich his life as much as his inner worlds do. He needs to reconnect with his body and be pushed into physical activity.

What happened to him at an early age to make this archetype dominate his personality? Were his parents reclusive? Did he have friends growing up? Did he live in an isolated area and never learn how to be with people? Was his mother always afraid of the city and couldn't be around people?

To grow, this archetype is best paired with one of the following:

❂ **The Fool**—can teach him how to have fun and to let loose. He can show him how to talk to people and rejoin life.

✪ **The Dictator**—would enforce so many rules and regulations that the Recluse would have to stand up for himself or give up his isolated lifestyle to follow another man's rule.

✪ **The Maiden**—would teach him how to love and what it means to be as playful and innocent as a child. Her adventurous nature could change his entire life.

✪ **The Scorned Woman**—would be so hurt by her past relationships that she would outdo him in her antisocial behavior. He would probably see himself mirrored in her and decide to change his ways.

THE RECLUSE

Assets:

- Prefers to be left alone most of the time.
- Longs for the next project or idea to occupy his time.
- Could easily live the life of a monk.
- Has a rich inner life.
- Is psychically sensitive.
- May long for a small family unit.
- Can be philosophical and highly intelligent.
- Can be a very loyal companion.
- Can be reliable since he's always in the same place.
- Doesn't play the games people play or get involved in their dramas.
- Is very discerning.

Flaws:

- Is unexpressive and able to withdraw easily.
- Is afraid of his emotions and seems devoid of feeling.
- Has trouble talking to people.
- Is very pessimistic.
- Holds grudges.

Robert Louis Stevenson created a character that shows both sides of the Hades archetype: Dr. Jekyll represents the Recluse; Mr. Hyde represents the Warlock.

The Villainous Side of the Recluse: The Warlock

As a villain the Recluse becomes the Warlock. He uses his knowledge of the occult to harm others or the environment. He's out for his own personal gain and understands nothing of the effect his actions have on the outer world. He has spent so much time studying esoteric ideas he is drawn to test them out.

His loneliness may also lead him to a schizoid existence where his fantasies cause him to do harm to others.

He has a tendency to avoid people and social situations. He's so afraid of rejection he never shows anyone his work or tells them his ideas. He has no close relationships, is inhibited and socially inept, and is reluctant to take risks.

He doesn't understand why it's so bad to want to be alone. He doesn't want to be a part of society because people are killing each other every day. Spirits are his company. Their world is fascinating to him and they teach him things. He can cast spells to make others leave him alone if he wants to. He is very into the occult and all things antiestablishment. He likes it when others are afraid of him so they'll leave him alone.

THE WARLOCK

- Is antisocial.
- Is out for his own gain.
- Doesn't care how his actions affect the world.
- May experiment with the occult to gain power.
- Is afraid of rejection.
- Has no intimate relationships.
- Can't feel or express real love without dominating the other person.
- Thinks society is a joke and that he doesn't have to live under its rules.
- Wants to be in control.
- Likes to intimidate others.

Hades in Action

Recluse/Warlock TV Heroes

Angel (David Boreanaz) in *Buffy the Vampire Slayer* and *Angel*

Fox Mulder (David Duchovny) in *The X-Files*

Recluse/Warlock Film Heroes

Rick Blaine (Humphrey Bogart) in *Casablanca*

Jerry Fletcher (Mel Gibson) in *Conspiracy Theory*

Jim Stark (James Dean) in *Rebel Without a Cause*

Lo (Chen Chang) in *Crouching Tiger, Hidden Dragon*

Crash Davis (Kevin Costner) in *Bull Durham*

Recluse/Warlock Literary and Historical Heroes

Beast in *Beauty and the Beast*

Daniel Boone

the Phantom in *Phantom of the Opera*

Hamlet in *Hamlet* by William Shakespeare

Heathcliff in *Wuthering Heights* by Emily Brontë

Rochester in *Jane Eyre* by Charlotte Brontë

Holden Caulfield in *The Catcher in the Rye* by J.D. Salinger

Dr. Hannibal Lecter in *The Silence of the Lambs* by Thomas Harris

George Emerson in *A Room With a View* by E.M. Forster

Victor Frankenstein in *Frankenstein* by Mary Shelley

Kurtz in *Heart of Darkness* by Joseph Conrad

Quasimodo in *The Hunchback of Notre Dame* by Victor Hugo

Daryl Van Horne in *The Witches of Eastwick* by John Updike

Roderick Usher in "The Fall of the House of Usher" by Edgar Allan Poe

Philip Marlowe in novels by Raymond Chandler

Byronic heroes

Dr. Jekyll and Mr. Hyde in *The Strange Case of Dr. Jekyll and Mr. Hyde* by Robert Louis Stevenson

Chapter 14

Hermes
The Fool and the Derelict

Dancing through life, the fool lives without a care in the world. He exists between the world of adults and the world of children. All of life is simple, light and amazing to him. He wanders from place to place looking for a new playmate—whether it be a person, a dog or a game doesn't matter to him. His heart is full of love and laughter. He is the most playful of all the gods and often acts as a messenger between humans and the gods as he loves adventures and travel.

The Fool

The Fool is a man who is still a boy inside. He won't grow up and doesn't feel inferior to others; he thinks they're somewhat blind to their own boring and shallow existences. People often flock around him after work because they know he'll lead them to the party where they can unwind.

He enjoys playing around and not acting his age. He thinks stressed-out businessmen are just plain crazy. He believes life should be fun and he's determined to enjoy himself. And he doesn't need a big fancy house with an expensive car in the driveway to do it.

He avoids commitments and romantic entanglements. The women in his life must respect this if they want to be around him.

He loves to be the go-between, circulating through many social cliques. He doesn't care if what he's doing is legal or not. The consequences of his actions aren't important to him because he lives in the moment as a free spirit. He won't go as far as to hurt someone, but that's his only moral code. He'll

Don Quixote exhibits some of the qualities of the Fool archetype with his idealistic energy and his reliance on the imagination.

try anything once, and the more people present to witness his actions the better. He'd make a great salesman or actor because he loves to be the center of attention and doesn't want to be tied down to a nine-to-five job. He's a wanderer at heart and makes new friends wherever he goes.

What Does the Fool Care About?

❂ The Fool cares about his freedom. He loves to come and go as he pleases and often disappears for days or weeks at a time. He's always looking for the next adventure. The newness of the experience gets to him.

❂ He enjoys a challenge in all areas of his life and has no trouble being alone.

❂ He cares about remaining youthful and carefree no matter what his age.

❂ He cares about children and will risk his life to save them because he identifies with their innocence.

What Does the Fool Fear?

✪ The Fool fears losing his freedom. Being stuck in bed or in a prison would be devastating for him, and he'd do anything to avoid it; he'd risk death to escape it.

✪ He also fears boredom; he'll come up with a way to amuse himself with a rubber band if that's all he has. He's the first one to talk his friends into cutting school to go hang out.

✪ He loves to be risky. Hang gliding off the Twin Towers is his idea of fun. His young attitude makes him feel invincible, and he's addicted to the rush of adrenaline.

✪ He never makes commitments, at least not ones he can't walk away from easily.

✪ He loves to help children and fears not being able to save them when they're in trouble. He's still a child himself no matter what his age is. He understands children and their capacity to play, create and inquire.

What Motivates the Fool?

✪ His biggest motivator is the need to know and understand. He keeps his mind working as well as his body. His inquisitiveness drives his adventures forward and offers variety and spice to his life.

How Do Other Characters See the Fool?

✪ Others see him as either unpredictable and fascinating or childish and flighty. He has energy that never seems to stop and exudes an enthusiasm that can drive others crazy as he comes up with yet another new idea. No one can remember what his latest project is because he changes it so often.

✪ He's often dressed in casual clothes or the latest teen fad regardless of his age.

✪ His imagination always seems to be working, and he

Uncle Remus's capacity to understand children and his love for storytelling are both qualities of this archetype.

often has a distant look on his face when others fall into deep serious conversations near him.

Developing the Character Arc

Look at your character's main goal in the story and then at the fears you've selected to use against him. What does he need to learn to help him overcome his fear? Does he need to find a job to support a relative? Does he need to deal with a terminal illness? Has he been drafted? Was he accused of a crime he didn't commit?

Very often the Fool needs to learn to set limits on his behavior. He doesn't realize how much pain he can cause people in his wake. He needs to consider their feelings if he is to have any relationships at all, especially with his family. He also needs to learn how to take care of himself and accept some responsibility for his behavior. He must learn to respect the authority of the King or he'll suffer the consequences.

What happened to him at an early age to make this archetype dominate his personality? Did his parents fight all the time and he tried to lighten things up by being the comedian? Was he glorified for being the class clown or the derelict? Did his father yell all the time and he had to learn how to talk his way out of trouble? Were his parents adventurous?

To grow, this archetype is best paired with one of the following:

 ○ **The Businessman**—can teach the Fool responsibility and about how to take care of himself as adults do.

 ○ **The Abuser**—a father could take all the fun out of the Fool's life by pushing him to grow up and take care of himself so he can leave home.

 ○ **The Matriarch**—would teach him about family and commitment. He'd learn that to be totally without roots is to be totally alone.

 ○ **The Destroyer**—would change his life and make him wake up to the fact that he can be an adult and still have fun.

THE FOOL

Assets:
- Loves to play practical jokes.
- Is easygoing.
- Is adventurous and inquisitive.
- Can go on adventures alone.
- Is charming and playful.
- Has a strong imagination and is always full of ideas.
- Acts and dresses young for his age.
- Hates to plan things ahead of time and is very spontaneous.
- Can be a wonderful friend, focused on only you when he's around.
- Loves children because he's youthful himself.

Flaws:

- Is impulsive and reckless, without limits.
- Is terrified of commitment.
- Can pick up and disappear for long stretches of time.
- Takes extreme risks because he feels invincible.
- Can't handle responsibility or a traditional job.

The Villainous Side of the Fool: The Derelict

As a villain the Fool becomes the Derelict. He often will be found among the con men on city streets hustling for cash. He has great charm and charisma that draws people to his games. His smile makes him appear to be trustworthy as he engages them in conversation.

He does everything in excess and causes his parents and family a lot of misery and shame. He doesn't consider the consequences of his actions and may be arrested for his actions. Every parent dreads the late-night phone call, but for his parents it's a common occurrence. If his parents are well-off socially this can be a huge problem, and they may disown him. This only gives him more reason to feel slighted and abandoned and begin acting out even more for attention.

He has a pattern of irresponsible behavior that lacks morals and ethics. He's self-centered when it comes to his problems. "No one else matters but me" is his mantra. He believes he is special and above the law and feels entitled to be around others he views as unique and special. He can be arrogant and can lack empathy toward others.

He doesn't understand why he should have to listen to authority figures. He feels they have no right to boss him around. He thinks of his father as purely a sperm donor with a checkbook. He wants to be his own man. He thinks, "Just because their lives are boring doesn't mean mine has to be. I want to have fun and make my own rules."

THE DERELICT

- Is like an expert con man, hustling for a quick buck.
- Hates authority figures and views his father as a checkbook.
- Doesn't care about other people's feelings.
- Is an embarrassment to his family.
- Is self-centered.
- Is irresponsible and lacks ethics.
- Feels above the law.
- Lacks empathy.
- Is arrogant and confrontational.
- Easily succumbs to addictions.
- Expects others to bail him out of a crisis.
- Runs when the going gets tough.

Hermes in Action
Fool/Derelict TV Heroes

Joey Tribbiani (Matt LeBlanc) in *Friends*
Gilligan (Bob Denver) in *Gilligan's Island*
Cosmo Kramer (Michael Richards) in *Seinfeld*
Xander Harris (Nicholas Brendon) in *Buffy the Vampire Slayer*
Lou Costello in *Abbott and Costello*
Warren "Potsie" Weber (Anson Williams) and Ralph Malph (Don Most) in *Happy Days*

Fool/Derelict Film Heroes

Joel Goodson (Tom Cruise) in *Risky Business*

Jay (Will Smith) in *Men in Black*

Austin Danger Powers (Mike Myers) in *Austin Powers: International Man of Mystery*

Chon Wang (Jackie Chan) in *Shanghai Noon*

Buck Russell (John Candy) in *Uncle Buck*

Fool/Derelict Literary Heroes

Uncle Remus in *The Complete Tales of Uncle Remus* by Joel Chandler Harris

Don Quixote in *Don Quixote of La Mancha* by Miguel De Cervantes

Peter Pan in *Peter Pan* by James Barrie

Puck in *A Midsummer Night's Dream* by William Shakespeare

Tom Sawyer in *The Adventures of Tom Sawyer* by Mark Twain

the Fool in *King Lear* by William Shakespeare

Chapter 15

Dionysus
The Woman's Man
and the Seducer

Underneath the full moon, Dionysus dances with the women from town. As the only man present, he joins with his own feminine nature and holds the attention of all the women present. He serves them wine, intoxicating and loosening them up. Even the old and quiet women find themselves rejoicing around him, shedding their harsh self-images for more positive and fun ones. He brings out the best in them and shows them the best in himself. Together they experience moments of ecstasy and joyous madness.

The Woman's Man

The Woman's Man is a man who genuinely loves women. They captivate him. He isn't necessarily effeminate and can be very masculine. He simply loves everything about women and views them as equal or better than himself. He worships women and has stronger friendships with them than he does with other men. He'll never be one of the guys and cares nothing about the old boys' network.

Women love him; his free spirit is an inspiration. He encourages women to be strong, tough and sensual. Many women are forever changed by his friendship and often leave bad relationships because of the strength he gives them. He's a best friend to women. He transforms women into strong beings with higher self-esteem. All women are beautiful to him, and he tells them so often. Beneath it all he may be hiding a need to find the idealized woman who can be both a wife and a mother to him, but this is impossible for him.

Eventually he'll move on, unable to commit to any one woman. This is when most women realize he was only the catalyst to find their inner strength, and they don't need him to feel complete.

He understands women, and they love to take care of him. Often he is highly psychic and loves to play in other dimensions and altered states.

What Does the Woman's Man Care About?

❂ The Woman's Man cares about ecstasy, fun, sex and love. All acts of pleasure are his rituals. He gravitates to the quiet woman in the room in order to loosen her up.

❂ He loves to dream but can't commit to one goal. He craves the experience of the dream; it helps him think he has goals in a world where men are supposed to be goal driven. He is often persecuted by other men for being different.

❂ He cares deeply for his female friends and can't stand to see other men hurt a woman.

❂ He strives to be part of the counterculture, to live the life of a rock star. He can be a wonderful Shaman, as he loves to work in other realms and dimensions.

What Does the Woman's Man Fear?

❂ The Woman's Man fears being persecuted by society for not being man enough. Any job, whether he's in an office all day or working outdoors, would be torture. He can't follow rules or structure of any kind. Teaching esoteric or philosophical ideas may be one of the few jobs he's suited for.

❂ Losing his female friendships would devastate him. He needs to have women in his life.

❂ Experience is everything to him. He wouldn't mind being in a wheelchair for the rest of his life if he still had his

Porthos, one of Alexander Dumas's Three Musketeers, displays qualities of a Woman's Man through his swashbuckling nature and love for women.

freedom to go places.

๑ He fears having his dreams exposed as fantasies that will never come true. He's not into power and money but can't stand it when men who are pick on him for his values.

What Motivates the Woman's Man?

๑ His biggest motivators are love and belonging. The most important thing in his life is to be loved and needed by women. He feels connected when he's with a woman. He can give many women unconditional love at the same time whether he's sexual with them or not.

❂ His passion for esoteric ideas can spark his desires as well.

❂ Gambling or the idea of winning the lottery would be the most amazing thing he could imagine. It would give him total freedom to be himself without worrying about where he'll sleep next, and if he has money then other men won't look down on him but be envious of him.

How Do Other Characters See the Woman's Man?

❂ Others see him as a dreamer or a hippie, someone on the fringe of society.

❂ He's sometimes moody, laughing one minute and crying the next, but the way he does it makes most women see him as sensitive.

❂ He can wear anything, thrift store or Armani. He may not be attractive physically, but his essence and sensitivity are very attractive to women.

❂ He's very sensual and erotic and can often see inside a woman straight to her pain and desires.

❂ He's a great conversationalist.

Developing the Character Arc

Look at your character's main goal in the story and then at the fears you've selected to use against him. What does he need to learn to help him overcome his fear? Does he need to make male friendships or find male mentors? Does he need money to help his mother? Does he have a gambling or drinking problem that forces him to stop partying? Does he need to protect a woman from harm? Is he trying to find the perfect idealized woman who can be both a wife and mother to him?

Very often the Woman's Man needs to learn how to have men as friends. He needs male role models so he can grow up and see value in being male. Only then can he commit wholly

In *Shakespeare in Love,* Will Shakespeare's (Joseph Fiennes) free-spirited nature, love for women and passion for art make him an example of a **Woman's Man.**

to one woman. Very often this man lost his mother when he was young and is on a search to find a woman who can fill her shoes, which is virtually impossible.

He needs to stop running away from the responsibility of life. Every day is a party for him, but he can only keep such a lifestyle up for so long until it comes crashing down around him.

What happened to him at an early age to make this archetype dominate his personality? Did his mother die when he was young? Did he have a lot of nurses and female teachers who were nice and caring? Was his father mean to him or gone all the time at work? Was he shy and girls took to him? Was he uncoordinated and couldn't play sports with other boys and learn to be like them?

To grow, this archetype can be paired with one of the following:

✪ **The Businessman**—can teach the Woman's Man how to

be a part of the boys' club as well as provide him with a male role model.

○ **The Dictator**—can force the Woman's Man into taking responsibility for his life, or he can cause the Woman's Man to stand up for himself and fight it out.

○ **The Nurturer**—can take care of him and wait until he's ready for commitment. She is his dependable rock.

○ **The Femme Fatale**—can love him and leave him just as he seems to do to other women. He may fall in love with her for her independence and sensuality and then learn what it's like to be dumped.

THE WOMAN'S MAN

Assets:

- Shuns money and power for freedom and dreams.
- Loves all women regardless of appearance.
- Is chivalrous and gentle.
- Was close to his mother as a child, although she may have passed away when he was young.
- Loves to experience new things in life.
- Is erotic and sensual.
- Is looked down on by other men for his free lifestyle.
- Is psychic or into the paranormal.
- Is a smooth talker with a sharp wit.
- Is very supportive and always ready to offer his advice.

Flaws:

- Needs to be around women.
- Has trouble maintaining male friendships.
- Has trouble committing to women and career goals.
- Is searching for the impossible ideal of a woman who can be both his mother and his wife.

- Is irresponsible and flighty.
- Can be unambitious and unmotivated.

The Villainous Side of the Woman's Man: The Seducer

If the Woman's Man is hurt or betrayed by a woman, he may turn into the Seducer. As the Seducer he lures women away from good as well as bad relationships, causing havoc in their lives and leaving them alone to pick up the pieces when he's finished with them.

He has a pattern of excessive emotionalism and attention seeking. He has a low tolerance for problems and has rapidly changing emotions behind a face that remains stoic and un-readable. He's a ticking time bomb that no one knows about until he explodes. He is exceedingly sensitive to criticism and is overly concerned with his appearance.

He may become a stalker, obsessing about the one woman who won't return his favors. His dreams turn to fantasies about her, and he acts out his hurt on her.

He thinks he displays intense love for a woman. He feels he treats them well, and they owe him something. He does everything for them, risks everything for them, and if they want to leave him he won't stand for such treatment. He feels that "no other man is there for them like I am."

THE SEDUCER

- May be a stalker if rejected.
- Loves to play head games with women, coming on strong and then leaving them cold.
- Likes to be the one to end relationships.
- Often ends relationships when the woman seems to love him the most.
- Will be with several women at once and often chooses

to be with friends and sisters at the same time to create more turmoil in their lives.
- Feels entitled to attention from the women he helps.
- Thinks when a woman says no she's deliberately trying to hurt him—he'll show her who's boss.
- Is a ticking time bomb no one knows about until it's too late.
- Is extremely sensitive and can't handle rejection.
- His face remains stoic, not giving away his anger to warn anyone.
- Often mistakes obsession with love.

Dionysus in Action
Woman's Man/Seducer TV Heroes
Sam Malone (Ted Danson) in *Cheers*
Jesse Katsopolis (John Stamos) in *Full House*
Will Truman (Eric McCormack) in *Will & Grace*
Chandler Bing (Matthew Perry) in *Friends*

Woman's Man/Seducer Film Heroes
Nick Marshall (Mel Gibson) in *What Women Want*
Robbie Hart (Adam Sandler) in *The Wedding Singer*
Harry Burns (Billy Crystal) in *When Harry Met Sally*
Ted Stroehmann (Ben Stiller) in *There's Something About Mary*
Johnny Castle (Patrick Swayze) in *Dirty Dancing*
Dex (Donal Logue) in *The Tao of Steve*
Nickie Ferrante (Cary Grant) in *An Affair to Remember*
Ferris Bueller (Matthew Broderick) in *Ferris Bueller's Day Off*
Roger Thornhill (Cary Grant) in *North by Northwest*

Will Shakespeare (Joseph Fiennes) in *Shakespeare in Love*
Jack Dawson (Leonardo DiCaprio) in *Titanic*

Woman's Man/Seducer Literary and Historical Heroes

Count Vronsky in *Anna Karenina* by Leo Tolstoy
Count Dracula in *Dracula* by Bram Stoker
Mikhail in *Dark Prince* and *Dark Gold* by Christine Feehan
Leo in *I Know This Much Is True* by Wally Lamb
Billy the Poet in *Welcome to the Monkey House* by Kurt
   Vonnegut
John Willoughby in *Sense and Sensibility* by Jane Austen
Alec d'Urberville in *Tess of the d'Urbervilles* by Thomas
   Hardy
Porthos in *The Three Musketeers* by Alexander Dumas

Chapter 16

Osiris

The Male Messiah and the Punisher

Surrounded by light, Osiris walks across the earth carrying transformation and wisdom wherever he goes. He illuminates all he comes into contact with. He is the divine child and the divine consort. Killed by his own brother, he relied on his sister Isis to resurrect him. He loves humans so much that he sacrifices himself every year, giving the earth his body in winter and being reborn again in spring. He is life and death.

The Male Messiah

The Messiah is the archetype of androgyny. Both the male and female version of this archetype are identical except for the fact that the male preaches and shows the way to love and enlightenment while the female is the way to love and enlightenment.

The Male Messiah archetype can also contain any of the other archetypes, which will help him to achieve his goals in this lifetime. For example, William Wallace (Mel Gibson) in *Braveheart* is a savior of his people who embodies the Ares/Protector archetype to go to war and achieve his goal of freedom.

Also, the Male Messiah may not know of his connection to the Divine, but he may just be driven to accomplish something important. In this respect he isn't working on a spiritual goal. It seems his whole life is for one purpose and that purpose affects the lives of thousands of people. Think of Jeffrey Wigand (Russell Crowe) in *The Insider*, who gives up his wife, his

As Male Messiahs, Obi-Wan Kenobi (Alec Guinness) and Luke Skywalker (Mark Hamill) both seek to battle the evil of the dark side.

children and his career to fight the big tobacco companies. He may have been reluctant at first, but soon he realizes this is the reason he was born. He stands up, changes lives and finds his life purpose.

The Male Messiah has the ability to see the whole picture when it comes to problems. He never jumps to conclusions or gets involved in the gossip or drama of everyday life.

He respects all religions and belief systems. He gives freely of himself because he knows what he puts out comes back to him threefold.

The Male Messiah is more accepted by the masses as a spiritual authority figure because of his gender. He has the opportunity and ability to speak out and be active about his views. But as a male he may be looked down upon if his message is about the feminine traits of love and compassion.

Robin Hood's stealing from the rich to feed the poor makes him an example of the Male Messiah archetype.

What Does the Male Messiah Care About?

❂ Being born male, the Male Messiah doesn't have first-hand knowledge about the inequalities that exist in the world, but if he is of a minority race he'll learn this lesson quickly and be concerned with creating harmony among all people—think of Malcolm X.

❂ He cares about himself as well as others. Every living thing is a manifestation of the Divine to him.

❂ He cares about others recognizing their own divine nature, and he wants to teach others how to become like him.

❂ He reveres healing the soul above healing the body. He can't take away the pain of another who needs to learn from his experience even though he may be a gifted healer.

❂ He may not realize his Divine connections but be born

with a strong pull toward a goal and a willingness to sacrifice himself for it.

What Does the Male Messiah Fear?

✪ The Male Messiah fears people will be led astray by those on the wrong path, or by their own desire to please the senses or dull the senses with mind-numbing activities.

✪ He fears he won't be taken seriously and his message will be devalued.

✪ He fears he'll run out of time to fulfill his mission or that he'll have to watch others suffer.

What Motivates the Male Messiah?

✪ The aesthetic need to be connected to something greater than himself motivates him as well as his pursuit to give and receive unconditional love.

✪ He must battle his demons to maintain his connection to the Divine. He must face temptation and hold fast to his beliefs.

✪ His sense of purpose is so strong he can do nothing else but reach his goal.

How Do Others See the Male Messiah?

✪ Others see him as either good or bad; there is no in-between. He may be accused of starting a cult.

✪ Many view him as either idealistic, crazy and on a power trip, or as divine, wise and giving.

✪ Many are jealous of his connection with the Divine, especially clergy who feel entitled to such a thing. Think of Jesus and his connection to God, which led him to be crucified by his own people.

In the Bible, David, a Male Messiah, defeated Goliath and helped lead the Israelites to victory against the Philistines.

Developing the Character Arc

The Male Messiah doesn't necessarily change in his character arc but instead grows stronger through his fears.

Look at your character's main goal in the story and then at the fears you've selected to use against him. What does he need to learn to help him overcome his fear? Does he need to learn to be centered in a crowd of angry people? Does he need to face ridicule? Does he need to sacrifice his sense of self to find God?

Very often the Male Messiah needs to learn to let go of the

outcome of events and trust the spirit who guides him. He needs to stick to his convictions and fully believe in himself no matter the outcome.

He needs to face his accusers and his own doubts. He needs to stand tall in the face of adversity and attack. He must strongly believe in himself to survive in the long run.

When did his goals and views become strong in his life and why? Were his parents spiritual people? Was he actively involved in religion as a child? Did he speak out for the injustices other kids at school suffered?

Most likely this archetype will help other characters to grow instead of growing himself.

✪ He may find companionship with the Mystic.

✪ And laughter with the Fool.

✪ The Businessman can be a great challenge for him.

✪ The Warlock can be a great adversary.

THE MALE MESSIAH
Assets:

- Questions authority.
- Is disciplined.
- Has a healthy sense of who he is.
- Stands up for his beliefs no matter the cost.
- Has a strong spiritual belief system to pull him through tough times.
- Is willing to sacrifice himself for the good of all.
- Renounces material possessions.
- Has an inner strength that never dies.

Flaws:

- Needs to learn about the inequalities in the world.
- Is strong willed.

• Tells people the truth even if it's harsh.
• Pushes people beyond their limits to help them grow.

The Villainous Side of the Male Messiah: The Punisher

The Male Messiah isn't really a villain in the sense of being out for his own gain and desires. He's a villain in the sense of protecting the highest good for all. As the Punisher he'll curse the man who has "fallen" to teach him a lesson. He wants to break the man's ego. He'll kill the man's spirit to transform him into his image.

He may try to justify himself to others but they'll never fully understand his power or the burden he carries. They view his reprimands as harsh and uncaring. Many will leave his side, unable to follow his rules and treatment. Meditating six hours a day seems harsh and silly to most; to the Punisher it's a necessary step to advance. He feels his word is law.

THE PUNISHER

• Gives harsh criticism to his followers.
• Will curse a man to teach him a lesson.
• Wants to break others' egos and spirits.
• Feels his word is law.
• Won't try to reassure others or play favorites.
• Feels the pain of transformation is necessary.
• Pushes people beyond their limits.

Osiris in Action
Messiah/Punisher TV Heroes

Jonathan Smith (Michael Landon) in *Highway to Heaven*
Eric Camden (Stephen Collins) in *7th Heaven*

Messiah/Punisher Film Heroes

Luke Skywalker (Mark Hamill) in *Star Wars*

Jeffrey Wigand (Russell Crowe) in *The Insider*

David Dunn (Bruce Willis) in *Unbreakable*

Neo (Keanu Reeves) in *The Matrix*

Francesco (Mickey Rourke) in *Francesco*

Ulysses Everett McGill (George Clooney) in *O Brother, Where Art Thou?*

Charles Foster Kane (Orson Welles) in *Citizen Kane*

Messiah/Punisher Literary and Historical Heroes

Ulysses

Gandhi

Robin Hood

David

William Wallace

Malcolm X

Martin Luther King

Superman

Jesus in *Paradise Lost* by Milton

Paul Atreides in *Dune* by Frank Herbert

Poseidon
The Artist and the Abuser

In the depths of the sea, Poseidon forever sets the course of fate on waters of emotion, raging waves one moment and calm tides the next. He is unpredictable, dangerous and intriguing all at the same time. His eyes hide a mystery no one can quite touch. Once you think you know him he changes. Once you think you have helped him through an emotion another one surfaces more intensely than the last. He can give abundance from the sea's riches or take your life for venturing across his waters.

The Artist

The Artist is a man who is in touch with his emotions but may not always be the master of them. He can channel his feelings into a creative act, or he can let them simmer under the surface without an outlet until he bursts, lashing out at everyone around him. He has a hard time fitting into a world that devalues men who express their emotions, and this adds to his insecurity and anger. Anger seems to be the only acceptable emotion he is allowed to express, yet his feelings run the gamut from love to rage.

Women are initially very attracted to him for his intensity but soon learn how volatile his emotions can be. If he brings this same intensity when making up after a fight he'll win her over again because he's full of passion.

He doesn't realize the strength his emotions hold. He's very spontaneous and alive. He can amuse himself for hours with a simple toy or switch from one activity to another without missing a beat. If he can learn to control his outbursts he can be a very healthy and vibrant person who deals well with stress and the complexities of life. If his emotions control him he feels completely out of sync with the world around him and becomes a time bomb capable of going off at any moment.

He may seem calm on the surface but he has strong creative juices flowing deep inside. He is very driven to express himself and his ideas; he's passionate and his creativity is always personal. If he creates something, it always holds a deep meaning for him.

He's very instinctual and loves to be out in nature. He probably liked to tell time by the sun as a child.

What Does the Artist Care About?

❂ The Artist cares about releasing his own emotions. He thinks he's the center of the universe. It doesn't matter who is around him or what they may be going through; his emotions come first.

❂ He cares what others think of him and his creative efforts. Rejection is like death. He may destroy a work of art he created if even one person doesn't like it.

❂ He wants to be treated as an equal to all the smarter men around him, but he isn't good at the business side of things and depends on them to help his career along. He cares about pleasing his boss or agent and may wait until he comes home to vent his true feelings.

❂ He cares about appearing in control and looking strong to others. He likes his rage, as he thinks it gives him power and prowess. He uses it as a protective shield, and he needs it to defend himself. He doesn't know how to react to someone without anger as fuel.

In Arthurian legend, the knight Tristan falls in love with his King's bride, Isolde. Even though it is due to a love potion, the effects can't be erased, and Tristan loses all control of his emotions, much like the Artist archetype.

✪ He can get behind a creative project and work for years without running out of steam. He is a born creator.

What Does the Artist Fear?

✪ The Artist fears being seen as inferior to other men who can hold their emotions inside as society expects men to do. He wants to be king of his castle but lacks the authority of the King.

✪ He fears himself. He doesn't want to be a tyrant but has trouble controlling his outbursts. He's terribly afraid of hurting the ones he loves. He's also afraid that someone will harm his loved ones, which would release the vengeful monster in him.

❍ Because he's not a good businessman he's afraid of missing out on big career-making deals. He's always watching to make sure no one else takes credit for his work.

❍ He also fears the creative block. He may have a family or business problem that stifles his creativity, and he may wonder if the muse has permanently left him.

What Motivates the Artist?

❍ His biggest motivator is survival. Every encounter feels like a threat to his survival. It's as if one wrong comment or opinion on his work will destroy his career.

❍ Everything is seen in the extreme with him. He constantly feels he is fighting for his very life. If his wife talks to another man he thinks she's going to leave him. He's driven to prove himself right in such cases but he often proves himself wrong instead.

❍ Whether or not he realizes how foolish he has been, he still has trouble trusting others. Revenge can be an obsession.

❍ He's driven to be somebody important.

How Do Other Characters See the Artist?

❍ Some may see him as neurotic and as having no boundaries, while others may see him as passionate, spontaneous and alive, an unpredictable joy to be around.

❍ He dresses in comfortable clothing that expresses his mood, and he usually lets his hair hang loose. He's the most expressive man at the party, waving his hands as he talks.

❍ With one stare he can put another man in his place. His eyes speak volumes.

Developing the Character Arc

Look at your character's main goal in the story and then at the fears you've selected to use against him. What does he need to learn to help him overcome his fear? Does he need to learn the ways of the business world? Does he need to learn to control his fears of his wife leaving him? Does he need to get over a creative block? Does he need to learn how to interact with people? Does he need to give up his need to control others?

Very often the Artist needs to learn to distance himself from his initial feelings on a situation. He needs to react in proportion to the reality of the situation as it is, not as he imagines it to be. He needs to see his access to emotions as an asset that can help his artistic career and to recognize how he feels before his emotions get the better of him.

What happened to him at an early age to make this archetype dominate his personality? Was his father a rage-a-holic? Did a teacher criticize his creative work? Was he never able to grasp math and logical thinking? Did he love to play in nature and tell time by the sun?

To grow, this archetype is best paired with one of the following:

○ **The Businessman**—can teach the Artist how to take care of and manage his own career and destiny. He can show him how to be organized and in control of his feelings.

○ **The Woman's Man**—can show the artist how to be sexual and sensual. He can teach him how to love women and to find his feminine side. He can make the artist feel ashamed for the way he overreacts to events in his life.

○ **The Seductive Muse**—can teach him how to get in touch with his body and how to feel pleasure and happiness instead of just pain. The love she instills in men can make him willing to change for her.

⊙ **The Troubled Teen**—can turn his world upside down, leaving when he is on a rampage. She won't enable him to be emotionally abusive to her. She'll force him to look at his actions.

THE ARTIST
Assets:
- Loves to create and change things.
- Is spontaneous and instinctual.
- Could be a great creative artist.
- Is full of passion and intensity.
- Loves his family and friends despite how he acts around them.
- Will seek revenge for a harm done to him or his family.
- Is very street-smart as opposed to book smart.

Flaws:
- Expresses himself without regard to the feelings of others.
- Has trouble controlling his emotions.
- Invades other people's boundaries.
- Takes things to extremes.
- Is obsessive and relentless in his need for revenge.
- Imagines situations to be worse than they really are.
- Is self-centered.

The Villainous Side of the Artist: The Abuser
When the Artist can't control his emotions he becomes a volatile and vindictive man. His sense of revenge is strong, and he'll never let it go until he feels satisfaction. It's as if his survival depends on an eye for an eye.

When his temper flares out of control, Stanley Kowalski (Marlon Brando) in *Streetcar Named Desire* is an example of the villainous side of the Artist archetype: the Abuser. He cannot control his volatile emotions and lashes out at his sister-in-law, Blanche DuBois.

He'll lash out in a rage at home without regard to anyone else's feelings. He loses all boundaries and often hurts those he cares for. If his sexual urge is strong he may rape a woman, not understanding the word "no." He's not out to hurt her from the start but gets caught up in his own emotions; he doesn't understand how she feels. He's very good at making up. He's the quintessential man who beats his wife and gives her flowers and promises afterward.

He's antisocial with irresponsible behavior lacking in morals and ethics. He exhibits unlawful reckless behavior, refusing to conform to social norms. He seems to have no remorse and shows no thought for the consequences of his actions. He is physically aggressive, erratic and irritable, and disregards the safety of himself and of others.

He feels justified in his actions because he feels his basic rights have been violated. He doesn't care what anyone else thinks, and he'll destroy himself before he lets anyone else do it.

THE ABUSER

- Beats his wife and then brings her flowers to apologize.
- Plays head games with people.
- Is irritable and unpredictable.
- Is a ticking time bomb.
- Disregards the safety of himself and of others.
- Can't control his emotions and flies off the handle.
- Is driven to revenge and will hold a grudge for years.
- Has no boundaries.
- Doesn't understand the word "no" because he always gets his way.
- Is reckless and full of rage.

Poseidon in Action
Artist/Abuser TV Heroes

Bobby Donnell (Dylan McDermott) in *The Practice*
Jack McFarland (Sean Hayes) in *Will & Grace*
Chris Stevens (John Corbett) in *Northern Exposure*

Artist/Abuser Film Heroes

Jim Stark (James Dean) in *Rebel Without a Cause*

Boss Paul Viti (Robert De Niro) in *Analyze This*

Larry (Billy Crystal) in *Throw Momma From the Train*

J.D. (Brad Pitt) in *Thelma and Louise*

Artist/Abuser Literary and Historical Heroes

Vincent Van Gogh

Tristan in Arthurian legend

Angel Clare in *Tess of the d'Urbervilles* by Thomas Hardy

Othello in *Othello* by William Shakespeare

Queequeg in *Moby Dick* by Herman Melville

Stanley Kowalski in *A Streetcar Named Desire* by Tennessee
Williams

Tom Buchanan in *The Great Gatsby* by F. Scott Fitzgerald

Dad in *Angela's Ashes* by Frank McCourt

Will Ladislaw in *Middlemarch* by George Eliot

Prospero in *The Tempest* by William Shakespeare

Yuri Zhivago in *Doctor Zhivago* by Boris Pasternak

Chapter 18

Zeus
The King and the Dictator

High up on the mountain, Zeus surveys his land and castle. He looks down on those around him, making sure everything is in quiet order. Everywhere one turns, his watchful gaze can be felt; his power lingers long after he has left the area. He fills the sky with his image and demands respect. Beautiful women have no chance to tell him "no" as he is a forceful and sneaky lover, often disguising his true self to them. He can be your best friend one minute and your worst enemy the next. His wife Hera is the only one who can force him into things, often because she has the power to make his home life a living hell.

The King

Unlike the Male Messiah who sees the whole picture and knows how everyone will be affected by his actions, the King sees only the big picture (which ignores the details) and is unable to see how a decision he makes will affect others on a smaller scale.

He's without emotion and fills that void inside with addictions such as caffeine, work, alcohol and sex. The King is somewhat like a Godfather or a mobster boss who lives in excess. There's no middle ground for him in anything.

He's a very strong man who can lead armies to victory and motivate people with his character and charm. He's a great strategist who can relate to other men and offer them exactly what they want to come over to his side. His word is law but he'll allow other men the option of saving face in front of him.

He loves coming to the rescue of women regardless of

what his wife may think. Since he's devoid of emotion and guilt he can easily cheat on his wife and go right home to her again. If he's caught in the act he's more upset with himself for slipping up than for what he has done or how much he's hurt his family. He sees himself as having a separate life when he's out of the house. He provides for his family, protects them and feels entitled to the spoils of life. He'd make a great politician.

What Does the King Care About?

◉ The King cares about having a kingdom to rule over. He wants to have a family, a company or group to call his own.

◉ He cares about being admired and respected for his power and the fear he can instill in others when needed. He wants to be a strong force to reckon with.

◉ He cares deeply about those under his command and is extremely loyal and generous with them. Since he's unable to express his emotions toward them, he uses money and gifts instead.

◉ He also cares about being the best and will duel with his competition to earn that title no matter what the cost.

What Does the King Fear?

◉ The King fears someone stronger, younger, faster and smarter will come along and knock him down. He's worked hard to get to the top of the mountain in business and at home and is always on guard to keep his kingdom. He's much like a mob boss in this regard, and he fears losing his edge.

◉ He fears his own emotions because they're so foreign to him. He may desire a wife to express emotions for him. The more she cries the more he can watch her and hold his own tears at bay. Emotions are a sign of weakness to him and have no place in building a dynasty.

What Motivates the King?

✪ The King's biggest motivator is self-esteem and self-respect. He wants recognition for who he is. He wants his name alone to invoke respect in others and will do anything it takes to protect his image. All one has to do is dare him or call him a coward and he'll attempt anything, often pushing beyond what was dared.

✪ He expects his family and girlfriends to respect him as well. As a loving father he would be crushed by a daughter who rebels against him, often cutting her off completely.

✪ He'll do anything to maintain power.

How Do Other Characters See the King?

✪ Other characters either look up to him as a role model or see him as an egomaniac. His need for control dominates his life, and he'll clash with others who aren't as driven as he is. He doesn't have time for friendly nights on the town with regular friends who aren't a strong alliance for him.

✪ He is seen as unemotional—a rock. Nothing seems to faze him and weaker people going through a difficult time will often seek out his strength. Women in violent relationships may come to him for help, and his wife will feel as if she's lending her husband out to these women.

✪ He can be a sharp dresser, especially if it means outdoing a man more powerful than him. If that man has a $1,200 suit then he'll buy a $2,000 suit.

✪ He always comes off as being very confident and sometimes arrogant.

Captain Kidd is an
example of a historical
King archetype.

Developing the Character Arc

Look at your character's main goal in the story and then at the
fears you've selected to use against him. What does he need
to learn to help him overcome his fear? Does he need to learn
to express his emotions and find his heart? The King is very
much like the mob boss in *The Sopranos* who hides his feelings
so much he gets anxiety and can't be an effective boss until
he finds and expresses his pain. Does he need to let go of
control and domination and let someone else lead? Does he
need to face old age and competition from younger kings?

Very often the King needs to feel vulnerable to change. Something traumatic must happen to him or someone he's very close to so the wall he has built around his heart can break down. Sometimes he will literally have a heart attack.

What happened to him at an early age to make this archetype dominate his personality? Was his father weak or strong? Did his mother dominate him, making him feel like less of a man? Did the local bully beat him up until he fought back, almost killing the bully and therefore gaining power in school?

To grow, this archetype is best paired with one of the following:

○ **The Artist**—can help him find and express his emotions and show him how to be open to love and creativity.

○ **The Backstabber**—if the King loses a strong ally and friend his whole world may crumble, and he'd have to re-evaluate his entire life.

○ **The Amazon**—can show him that women can be great allies and friends. She can teach him that his feminine side doesn't have to be as weak as he thinks it is.

○ **The Femme Fatale**—the King thinks he's in total control of women and would be completely devastated if a woman got the better of him. The Femme Fatale can be sneakier and therefore more powerful than he is.

THE KING
Assets:
- Needs to have a family, group or company to rule over.
- Enjoys many activities and time away from his family.
- Is skilled at forming alliances.
- Spoils his friends and family with gifts.
- Is a great strategist.
- Can be very loyal and giving.

- Is very decisive and confident.
- Is the strongest man to lean on.

Flaws:
- Always needs to be in control of others; he loves to dominate.
- Feels entitled to a separate life outside of his family and marriage.
- Feels his wife should take care of all the day-to-day family issues so he won't be bothered.
- Enjoys instilling fear in others.
- Has trouble expressing emotions and sees them as weaknesses.
- Has trouble asking for help.
- Is very stoic and quiet.

The Villainous Side of the King: The Dictator

As a villain the King becomes the Dictator. His need to rule and control others becomes an obsession. He wants more and more control and submission over his subordinates. He'll even go as far as to punish innocents in order to send out a message that he's powerful. He wants to be a demigod, to have control over the destinies and lives of others to do with as he pleases.

If anyone stands up to him the beast will rage forth causing major destruction to anyone and everyone. He'll justify his behavior as being the fault of the one who stood up to him. "Everyone should know better than to defy me" is his mantra.

He makes up laws just for the sake of wielding his power. He loves to see people going out of their way to abide by his laws. He doesn't know the consequences of his actions and he doesn't care. "If everyone would just behave then I wouldn't have to be so demanding" is what he tells people when, in

In *Moby Dick*, as Captain Ahab becomes more obsessed with finding the whale, he displays characteristics of the Dictator archetype: an obsessive need to rule and a disregard for consequences.

fact, nothing could ever satisfy him.

He has passive/aggressive tendencies as well, where he'll tell a family member that it's OK if they do something he disapproves of, but his actions show them just the opposite. He controls what goes on in his kingdom and if the people don't like it, that's too bad. No one leaves his domain, especially not with a smile. Betrayal is the worst type of offense as far as he's concerned, and he will seek justice.

In *Treasure Island*, the characteristics of the villain Long John Silver are similar to the traits of the Dictator archetype.

THE DICTATOR

- Is obsessed by the need to control and rule others.
- Is passive-aggressive, allowing someone to make a mistake so he can punish them later.
- Can be a tyrant.
- Is a harsh wielder of justice.
- Creates meaningless laws just to wield power over people.
- Is extremely judgmental.

- Is frequently absent from his family's life.
- Instills fear in others by his name alone.
- Humiliates others and forces them to degrade themselves for mercy.

Zeus in Action
King/Dictator TV Heroes

Tony Soprano Sr. (James Gandolfini) in *The Sopranos*

Captain James T. Kirk (William Shatner) in *Star Trek*

Jerry (Jerry Seinfeld) in *Jerry Seinfeld*

Skipper Jonas Grumby (Alan Hale Jr.) in *Gilligan's Island*

Ricky Ricardo (Desi Arnaz) in *I Love Lucy*

Maurice Minnifield (Barry Corbin) in *Northern Exposure*

King/Dictator Film Heroes

Don Vito Corleone (Marlon Brando) in *The Godfather*

Don Michael Corleone (Al Pacino) in *The Godfather II*

Adam Bonner (Spencer Tracy) in *Adam's Rib*

General George S. Patton Jr. (George C. Scott) in *Patton*

King Mongkut of Siam (Yul Brynner) in *The King and I*

King/Dictator Literary Heroes

King Arthur

Julius Caesar

Long John Silver in *Treasure Island* by Robert Louis Stevenson

Captain Kidd

Captain Ahab in *Moby Dick* by Herman Melville

King Lear in *King Lear* by William Shakespeare

Big Daddy in *Cat on a Hot Tin Roof* by Tennessee Williams

Marc Antony in *Antony and Cleopatra* by William
Shakespeare

Tamburlaine in *Tamburlaine the Great* by Christopher
Marlowe

IV **Creating Supporting Characters**

Chapter 19

Introduction to Supporting Characters

Supporting characters are a great source to use to develop conflict within a story. In their own unique way each one of the supporting characters can create obstacles for the hero to overcome.

If your story is lagging in certain areas—a scene isn't working or a subplot is going nowhere—you can inject a supporting character to spice things up. These archetypes help you to create supporting characters with a life of their own and add color to your story. They don't just ask a question or say a line and walk away; they create memorable moments and add subtext to a scene. They hang around for a while, popping up at the worst moment to create new problems.

Think of Newman (Wayne Knight) from *Seinfeld* and all the times his hatred for Jerry made Jerry's life more miserable than it already was. Consider the episode where Jerry makes out in a movie theater during *Schindler's List* because his parents are staying in his apartment and he hasn't had any alone time with his girlfriend. The writers chose to put his enemy Newman in the theater at the same time so he could catch Jerry in the act. He causes trouble for Jerry by rushing home to tell Jerry's parents all about the spectacle Jerry made of himself with his girlfriend. This ultimately leads to Jerry not being able to see his girlfriend anymore.

As you work on the journey section and develop your plot, look for scenes or subplots that can use more tension or drama and try weaving a supporting character into the story.

There are three categories of supporting characters: Friends, Rivals and Symbols.

Chapter 20

Friends

Friends are supporting characters who mean well but sometimes cause trouble anyway. They can give wrong advice, forget to tell the hero something important, make the hero give up his quest in order to save them, or they may do something that works against the hero "for his own good."

There are four types of supporting Friends:

- The Magi
- The Mentor
- The Best Friend
- The Lover

The Magi

The Magi is the voice of wisdom. He's the all-knowing wise man who has been through what the hero is going through, possibly several times. He has the power to help the hero avoid problems and pitfalls but often sees the greater wisdom in having the hero figure things out for himself. "Experience is the greatest teacher" is the Magi's mantra. The Magi is the master teacher; the hero is the student.

The Magi is often unwilling to help the hero and prefers to be left alone like a hermit in a cave. The world and its problems aren't foremost on his mind. The Magi must be convinced to help, and the hero must see value in what the Magi has to offer. If the Magi decides to help the hero, he makes it clear that everything must be done as he says without question. His word is law.

The hero is often upset when she gets into trouble and

later learns the Magi could've easily helped her avoid it. She may not see the greater lesson she has learned until much later in the story when she faces a similar problem, only with more at stake. It is then she realizes she can "do this herself" and is able to overcome the situation on her own. If she hadn't experienced the first lesson she would be lost.

As their relationship grows the Magi often learns to like the hero as a friend or surrogate child. He can see himself in the hero and takes pleasure in living the newness of his craft through his student. As the hero succeeds he feels he has succeeded. If the student forgets the Magi or acts better than the Magi, things can go wrong in the relationship. The Magi may get upset that the hero is moving on without him, as if he's the baby being thrown out with the bath water.

The Magi can create conflict for the hero:

❍ By getting jealous of what the hero is accomplishing without him.

❍ By teaching the hero a harsh lesson, regardless of the hero's goal or time limits.

❍ By withholding information the hero needs to overcome a situation so she can learn on her own.

❍ By giving the hero the wrong information in order to teach her a lesson.

❍ By refusing to help at all.

Examples of the Magi:

❍ The Magi can be a master detective who knows all about the kinds of cases the hero is working on but has quit his job in order to forget all the brutality he saw. He doesn't take kindly to the new rookie coming to him for help and opening up all his memories again.

❍ The Magi can be the coach unwilling to train the new athlete.

✪ The Magi is often the master teacher of what the hero wants to master, whether it's martial arts, chess or something else.

The Magi in action:

✪ Obi-Wan Kenobi (Alec Guinness) in *Star Wars*

✪ Bruce Pandolfini (Ben Kingsley), the revered and respected chess teacher in *Searching for Bobby Fisher*

The Mentor

The Mentor is much more like the hero and closer to his level than the Magi. The Mentor freely offers advice and wants to be involved in the hero's problems. The Mentor is like an advanced helper who may soon need help himself.

The Negative Mentor

At his worst the Mentor loves the status and prestige he gets from his power to help the hero. He wants to be involved every step of the way and to hold onto his power over the hero. There is a hierarchy established, and the Mentor usually has a hard time letting go of it if the hero outgrows him. The greater the age difference, the easier it is for the Mentor to let go. If the hero is close to his age it can turn into a competitive relationship. The hero may see himself in the Mentor's eyes and may not like what his future may be. He may judge the Mentor for all the mistakes he has made and try to distance himself from him.

The Negative Mentor in action:

✪ Gordon Gekko (Michael Douglas) in *Wall Street*, the Wall Street tycoon who mentors and seduces the hero into dishonest trading practices.

✪ Katherine Parker (Sigourney Weaver) in *Working Girl*. She tells the hero to trust her and then gives the boss the hero's ideas as if they were her own.

The Positive Mentor

A good mentor will openly guide the hero on his quest and make herself available twenty-four hours a day. She'll see herself in the hero and enjoy reliving her past through him. She wants to give her advice and expertise. If the hero succeeds then so does the mentor. She feels no competition with the hero and at times seems very patient while the hero learns. Many times the mentor has a goal she never reached that's similar to the hero's goal. If she helps the hero she can reach that goal through him.

A lot of karate and action films follow this relationship, where the hero will successfully do what the mentor has never been able to do, be it winning a fight or finding the bad guy before he kills again—all with the mentor's help.

The Positive Mentor in action:

✪ Morpheus (Laurence Fishburne) in *The Matrix* knows he'll never be as skilled as Neo but he'll win the war with him.

✪ Mickey (Burgess Meredith) in *Rocky* knows he can't fight and never was as great as he can help Rocky to be.

✪

The Mentor can create conflict for the hero:

✪ By thinking he knows best (which he sometimes does), so he tries to reach the hero's goal himself, messing everything up in the process.

✪ By resenting the hero for growing past him and causing the hero emotional turmoil. He may leave the hero on his own just when he's needed the most. In this way the Mentor shows just how much he is needed.

✪ The hero may feel bad for the Mentor and allow him to come along, compromising the mission.

✪ The hero may become upset at having to leave the Mentor behind while he reaches for his goal and wastes valuable time in leaving. The hero sees himself years later in the Mentor's eyes.

Examples of the Mentor:

⊘ The old high school teacher the hero tracks down to ask advice.

⊘ Someone accomplished in the hero's line of work who takes him under his wing.

⊘ The expert on whatever information the hero needs, as long as he's excited to share the information and help.

The Best Friend

The Best Friend is the hero's confidant. She's the character who's always there, ready, willing but not always able to help. The Best Friend means well even if she messes up. She loves the main hero and wants to be there for her. If she sees the hero drifting away from her she'll try everything in her power to repair the friendship, even faking sickness to get attention. The Best Friend lives for this friendship whether she appreciates it in the beginning of the story or not.

Sometimes if the hero changes drastically, the Best Friend will feel threatened because she knows she must change with the hero or risk drifting apart from her. Some Best Friends don't like change.

The Best Friend can create conflict for the hero:

⊘ By giving bad advice without realizing it.

⊘ By not wanting the hero to change and outgrow her.

⊘ By being jealous of the hero's accomplishments and wishing she had the resources to be so heroic.

⊘ By steering the hero away from her goal and the right decision in order to keep her safe.

✪ By causing problems with and being jealous of the hero's relationships with other characters.

Think about how they met and how long they know each other. The Best Friend can be an unlikely match for the hero but there's usually some common ground between them. In *There's Something About Mary*, any character who had a mentally challenged sibling would be a friend of Mary's since Mary is so attached to her brother, who is mentally challenged.

How the hero and Best Friend came to know each other:

✪ The Best Friend can be in the same line of work or share the same interests as the hero.

✪ They may have met in grade school and have been friends since.

✪ They may have lived near each other and became good friends by geography alone, having no common interests.

✪ They may have met in work or college.

✪ They have only just recently met, and the hero doesn't know that much about her at all, adding mystery to their relationship.

The Best Friend in action:

✪ The Tin Woodman (Jack Haley) in *The Wizard of Oz* is the Best Friend to Dorothy; he doesn't provide much comic relief like the Scarecrow does, and he doesn't shadow her need for courage like the Lion does.

✪ The Droids in *Star Wars* are Luke Skywalker's best friends.

The Lover

The Lover is the love interest of the story. Even though some characters run from love out of fear, everyone ultimately wants to be loved and to fit in somewhere.

The Lover is home base and security. He's often the one the hero goes to to vent her feelings, especially her doubts and fears. The Lover is the silver lining among the clouds and may be the only character who believes in the hero at all. The Lover can come in the form of a pet, as in Toto from *The Wizard of Oz*, or the Lover can come in the form of a child for a parent.

The Lover can create conflict for the hero:

✪ By presenting the character with an ultimatum.

✪ By misunderstanding something and causing more trouble.

✪ By trying to help and instead messing things up even more.

✪ By getting caught by the bad guys and making the hero drop the goal to save the Lover.

If your hero falls in love with someone not deemed acceptable in the world of your story, that can cause a whole number of obstacles and subtext. How would the world or society of your story react to:

• A homosexual relationship?

• A relationship with extreme age differences?

• A relationship between different races?

• A relationship between two classes?

What kind of relationship do they have?

✪ The Lover can be the exact opposite of the hero, bringing balance into her life.

✪ The Lover can fill the void left by a parent if the hero didn't feel loved as a child.

✪ The Lover can be domineering and controlling or sensitive and easygoing.

✪ The Lover can play a small part in the hero's life until her world comes crashing down around her.

Think about how you introduce the Lover, in your story. The first time we meet the Lover, the relationship between him and the hero should be established. The Lover is the one character who demands a certain way of being treated. You wouldn't think badly of a hero who snubs her friend when she's busy, but you'd think badly of a hero who snubs her lover for any reason. The Lover is supposed to hold a special place with the hero; if he doesn't we need to know why, because it will tell us something about the hero's personality. If she treats him like a best friend then maybe she has trouble with commitment.

The Lover in action:

❂ Princess Leia (Carrie Fisher) in *Star Wars* is Luke Skywalker's love interest with a strong will of her own.

❂ Toto in *The Wizard of Oz* has Dorothy's unconditional love, and she risks all to save him.

Chapter 21

Rivals

Rivals are friendly adversaries out to "get" the hero. They dislike the hero but aren't the antagonists in the story because they don't oppose the hero's goal; they just create conflict and problems for the hero along the way. They don't mean harm but enjoy messing things up for the hero because it gives them something to do. They may even be upset if the hero wasn't there to "play" with any more. Think of Newman on *Seinfeld*.

Very often a rival's hatred for the hero is unconscious. He may think he's helping the hero to reach his goal, but in reality he's sabotaging every effort the hero makes. The Jester fits here nicely. He would unconsciously break things and ruin the "treasure map" before the hero finds the "treasure." Now the hero must find another way.

On the other hand, an enemy's hatred can be completely conscious, as in the case of the Nemesis, who waits for an opportunity to get even with the hero. Think of Carla (Rhea Perlman) on *Cheers*, who is always causing trouble for Diane (Shelley Long) when she has other problems to deal with.

Rivals may help out the antagonist at times but only up to a certain point. They relish their power to thwart the hero in his quest, but when it comes down to real danger and possible harm against the hero they'll often back away, not meaning to hurt anyone *that* much. It's just a friendly game to them.

All Rivals share the same reasons as to why they dislike the hero:

○ He could have always felt as if he's in competition with

the hero.

✪ He could be jealous of what the hero has and unconsciously doesn't want to see him attain more.

✪ He could feel as if the hero thinks he's better than him and set out to put him down at every opportunity.

✪ He can feel that he's justified in stopping the hero because his beliefs tell him the hero is wrong. He can believe that he's fighting for a greater cause.

✪ He can feel that he's smarter than the hero and knows best, and that it's his job to teach the hero a lesson.

✪ He could just enjoy holding power over the hero, like a taunting school bully.

There are six types of supporting rivals:

• The Joker
• The Jester
• The Nemesis
• The Investigator
• The Pessimist
• The Psychic

The Joker

The Joker is a troublemaker with a sharp wit. He loves to tell jokes about and play pranks on the hero. Life is laughter and fun to him. He basks in the attention a good joke brings him because it makes him feel like the center of attention.

He can be very obnoxious, loud and boisterous. Just when the hero is on the verge of a breakthrough, the Joker arrives and messes up the hero's thought processes with his jokes and games. Or just as another character is about to confess something really important, the Joker comes in and changes the conversation. He may not even realize he has done this. He thinks he's helping people to loosen up and "de-stress."

The Joker is somewhat self-absorbed because he only cares about laughter and levity—which is what he wants. If someone else is upset and trying to express her emotions, he'll interject comedy into the situation to make himself feel more comfortable. He can't be in a scene without making a joke, and someone had better laugh *with* him or he'll turn angry and say harsh things. Somehow he comes to know people's secrets and will use them as a weapon if he feels humiliated.

The Joker can create conflict for the hero:

✪ By needing so much attention that he drives the hero crazy.

✪ By causing the hero to go out of his way to avoid him so he loses an opportunity to attain the goal.

✪ By playing a joke on the hero that takes him further away from his goal.

✪ By giving others false information on the hero to cause more trouble between the hero and others.

The Joker in Action:

✪ Sam Malone in *Cheers* uses jokes about women to avoid intimacy.

✪ Darlene Conner (Sara Gilbert) in *Roseanne* uses nasty insulting jokes to get through her problems.

✪ Chandler in *Friends* uses jokes to avoid feeling his emotions and to stop others from being too serious when they want to discuss their problems.

The Jester

The Jester is similar to the Joker except she truly means well most of the time. She messes up the hero's plans with her physical mistakes. She's a supporting character who shares similarities with Lucy from *I Love Lucy* or Larry and Curly from the *Three Stooges*. She's a very uncoordinated risk taker. She has no problem with the idea of jumping out of an airplane, but as soon as she attempts it a physical catastrophe occurs.

The Jester tries to help the hero but winds up ruining everything. The hero feels obligated to let her help because she's so sincere and innocent. The hero can't tell her to go away because she feels bad for the Jester, who is often less fortunate. At some point the sparks will fly between them, especially when the hero is under a lot of stress and pressure.

The Jester can cause conflict for the hero:

○ By following the hero around and physically wreaking havoc everywhere.

○ By getting herself in trouble so the hero has to stop everything to help her.

○ By ignoring the hero when she finally does tell her to stay out of her way. She secretly causes trouble and may be angry with the hero for excluding her.

The Jester in action:

○ Joxer (Ted Raimi) in *Xena* never does anything right but manages to help distract the bad guys with his antics.

○ Cosmo Kramer in *Seinfeld*.

○ Leo Ketz (Joe Pesci) in *Lethal Weapon*.

○ Scarecrow (Ray Bolger) in *The Wizard of Oz* gets set on fire several times, falls apart literally and has trouble walking.

The Nemesis

The Nemesis isn't a villain but a "friendly" troublemaker, similar to Carla on *Cheers* and Newman on *Seinfeld*. He doesn't care much about the hero's goals; he's just waiting around for a chance to consciously mess things up for the hero. He has a civilized relationship with the hero for the sake of mutual friends or work or whatever it is that keeps them together, but things turn ugly as soon as they're alone together. The nemesis may be a little jealous of the hero. He wants to see the hero walk in his shoes for a change. He feels his life is so hard and trying that the "perfect" hero wouldn't last a day in his shoes.

The Nemesis passionately hates the hero, yet he can't seem to live without having the hero there to hate. Newman's life would be boring without having Jerry to hate, and Carla would have no one to battle with if Diane wasn't around. The Nemesis's identity is wrapped up in hating the hero. Very often this love/hate relationship has been going on for years and neither character can remember how it began. They just know they're supposed to hate each other, so they do. Sometimes they'll work together for a common goal, but as soon as the goal is achieved they part ways again. Mimi Bobek (Kathy Kinney) and Drew Carey in the *Drew Carey Show* often pair up to play a joke on someone else, like their mutual boss. Jerry teams up with Newman in an effort to help Newman get a job out of state and therefore out of Jerry's life.

The Nemesis can create conflict for the hero:

❂ By constantly being in the shadows waiting for the hero to slip up, which makes the hero feel more pressure.

❂ By stepping into the scene and creating a new obstacle every time the hero is close to his goal. If the hero is waiting for a phone call from the killer, the Nemesis will be there to answer the phone and aggravate the killer.

The Nemesis in action:

❂ Mimi in *The Drew Carey Show*.

❂ Carla in *Cheers*.

❂ Newman in *Seinfeld*.

The Investigator

The Investigator is always butting in when she's not wanted or needed, always asking questions and driving the hero crazy.

The Investigator is very insecure. She has to know every minute detail of a situation before making a decision on what to do. She's afraid of taking chances because she's afraid of being wrong. She may have a need to do everything "by the book" because she's so afraid of getting into trouble with the law.

She tries to control and manipulate the hero into doing what she wants her to do. She's very jealous of the hero accomplishing her goal because she may have a similar one. To see the hero do what she wishes she could do is painful for her, so she can't let the hero do it without facing all of the Investigator's fears for her. She uses questions such as "Well did you think about this . . ?" to throw doubt at the hero, implying the hero needs her.

At first the hero welcomes the questions as helpful, but at some point they grate on her nerves. She realizes what the Investigator is doing and tries to get rid of her.

The Investigator sometimes feels like the whole world is at stake and the hero owes it to everyone to be sure about her actions and decisions. The Investigator worries so much she stops everyone from taking a stand and acting.

The Investigator can cause conflict for the hero:

✪ By constantly throwing questions at her every step of the way, slowing down her progress.

✪ By sapping so much of the hero's energy by pulling her in different directions. The hero makes a decision and then the Investigator keeps making her run around in circles, changing her mind back and forth over it.

The Investigator in action:

✪ Danny's (John Candy) overbearing mother in *Only the Lonely*.

✪ In *The Awakening*, Madam Ratignolle reminds Edna that

she cannot live completely free of social constraints—that her actions have consequences.

The Pessimist

The Pessimist challenges the hero with his constant disapproval of the hero's actions. He has a "nothing will work" attitude and doesn't bother to ask questions like the Investigator. He knows nothing will go the way it should so he doesn't even try. He's the master of inaction and loves to see his doubts take over the hero's thoughts. When the hero is unsure of himself the Pessimist feels justified in feeling bad about everything. "He can't, we can't, it's impossible" is his mantra.

He doesn't know how to look at the bright side of things. He has no hope and thinks the hero is stupid for not worrying about outcomes. He says things like, "You could walk outside and get hit by a car and die for all you know and then what happens?" Risk taking isn't part of his routine unless he has a death wish. Then he takes risks hoping for a bad result.

The Pessimist can cause conflict for the hero:

⊙ By shooting down every idea the hero has one by one until the hero has no ideas left.

⊙ By causing the hero to doubt every action he has taken or will take.

⊙ By making the hero feel defeated before he has even begun to fight.

⊙ By making the hero make the wrong decisions.

⊙ By persuading the hero to not take any action until the stakes are raised so high he has to do something.

The Pessimist in action:

⊙ This character shows up a lot in historical stories where people do things above and beyond what has been done before. *Elizabeth* and *Malcolm X* had characters in them saying how dangerous and foolhardy it was for the main characters to continue on their paths. Robert the Bruce (Angus Mac-Fadyen) is an example of a pessimist in *Braveheart*.

The Psychic

A Negative Psychic:

At her worst the Psychic knows it all or at least thinks she does. She has a very superior attitude about everything. She tries to come across as calm and all knowing in every situation but often looks ridiculous. She tries to predict what will happen next, good or bad, and tells the hero what the antagonist is planning next.

Occasionally she is in the role of a detective, psychic or a psychologist who thinks she knows everything about human behavior. If her predictions turn out to be wrong she'll always have an external factor of some sort to blame. She feels that she should be in the hero's place because she is superior to her.

Most of the time she's just a character looking for power and a special place to be held in high regard as compared to the other characters. Being smart or mentally gifted makes her different, unique and sought after.

The Negative Psychic in action:

✪ Oda Mae Brown (Whoopi Goldberg) in *Ghost* stole money from people as a fake psychic, putting on elaborate shows for them.

The Positive Psychic:

At his best the Psychic is like an oracle who gives advice and information to help the hero on her path. He does what is best for the hero, not his own ego. He may not want recognition for his actions and can choose to stay behind the scenes, anonymous.

The Positive Psychic in action:

❂ Oracle (Gloria Foster) in *The Matrix* freely gives advice to all the characters and expects nothing in return. She's committed to the cause and fights for the greater good. She gives Neo the wrong advice because that is what he needs to hear.

❂

The Psychic can cause conflict for the hero:

❂ By withholding valuable information so she has more to contribute later.

❂ By trying to take over part of the mission and messing up the hero's plan of action.

❂ By insisting that she knows better than the hero and causing other characters to doubt the hero's plan.

❂ By scaring the hero or other characters with her predictions. She may tell the hero she has "seen" or "knows" that a certain action won't work and now the hero has more doubts to battle.

Chapter 22

Symbols

Symbol characters symbolize something important to the hero. They can be a symbol of the hero's past, the hero's faults or of who the hero is trying to become.

Sometimes a friend or enemy can take on the role of a symbol character, such as the Best Friend who mirrors the hero's flaws.

There are three types of supporting Symbols:
• The Shadow
• The Lost Soul
• The Double

The Shadow

The Shadow mirrors the hero's character flaws or dark side so he can confront and overcome his shortcomings. The hero will try to avoid the Shadow because he has to face his faults and fears around him. The Shadow is very much defined by his and the hero's shortcomings.

If your character has a hard time facing his fears, the Shadow can be the most fearful person in the universe. Shadows are usually exaggerated, fighting to be recognized and healed. If the hero is afraid of going crazy, the Shadow can be an insane person. If the hero is always angry, the Shadow can be a rageful person.

The Shadow also states what others are afraid to say. In horror films he's the one who shouts, "We're all gonna die!" In dramatic stories he's the father or mother figure the hero doesn't want to become.

The Shadow can cause conflict for the hero:

❂ By causing the hero emotional turmoil as he faces himself in the Shadow.

❂ By being a force equal to or greater than the hero so he can put up roadblocks until the hero acknowledges him. If the hero is angry, the Shadow's rage can interrupt the plan of action toward the goal.

The Shadow in action:

❂ All the terrified characters next to Laurie Strode (Jamie Lee Curtis) in *Halloween*.

❂ The Cowardly Lion (Bert Lahr) in *The Wizard of Oz* who symbolizes the courage Dorothy needs to find within herself.

The Lost Soul

The Lost Soul symbolizes the hero's past, reminding her where she came from and why she chose to change. The hero will fall back into being like the Lost Soul if she doesn't attain her goal. The Lost Soul is the before image, the one who has never reached her goal because she probably never thought about goals at all. She often lets life push her around, reacting to events instead of creating them. She doesn't know how to change her life and is terrified to take the first step. It isn't until she sees the hero that she realizes how far she hasn't gone in life. This may depress her. Often the hero may pick up on this and try to play down her accomplishments around the Lost Soul.

❂ She's the old friend from childhood who hasn't changed a bit and all the hero can talk to her about is the past.

❂ The Lost Soul can be the man who gave up his ambitions to support a family and isn't happy with his choice.

❂ He can be the kid on drugs who has grown up to be a

man on drugs while his friends have gone off to college to build careers.

⊘ The Lost Soul can also be the woman who gave up her career to raise kids and support a family while the hero gave up having kids for her career, or vice versa. The hero may have once been jealous of her but she now knows the Lost Soul's life isn't for her, and she couldn't imagine being her.

"There but for the grace of God go I" is what the hero thinks when she sees the Lost Soul. If she had chosen to remain passive and not go after her goal, she would be the Lost Soul. This supporting character can motivate the hero to accomplish her goal out of fear of becoming a Lost Soul herself.

The Lost Soul can create conflict for the hero:

⊘ By trying to convince the hero that her life is great and the hero made a big mistake in choosing her path in life.

⊘ By constantly being a reminder of who the hero was and still may become if things don't work out.

⊘ By making the hero feel guilty about her accomplishments.

⊘ By doing something drastic to get the attention and help of the hero at the worst possible time in the plot.

The Lost Soul in action:

⊘ George Costanza (Jason Alexander) in *Seinfeld* never wants to do anything but coast through life.

⊘ Madam Ratignolle in *Awakening* is the Lost Soul to Edna.

The Double

The Double is who the hero wants to become—a role model. The hero either admires the Double or is jealous and critical of him. The Double is who the hero wants to become when he attains his goal. He's well-rounded, secure and grounded.

Whatever interests the hero has—science, writing, art—the Double is the expert in that field and is usually unavailable or unreachable. The hero's interest is usually an integral part of the plot where such expertise will help him to attain his goal.

The hero may be trying to write a novel and dreams of becoming as successful as Stephen King. His whole bedroom may be filled with Stephen King novels. Or the hero may want to discover how to hack into a new computer system and would give anything to meet the great mysterious programmer/hacker that invented the security system he can't crack.

At their best Doubles become gurus or guides for the hero. They blaze a trail for the hero to follow or hold space for the hero to blossom on his own.

The Double can create conflict for the hero:

✪ By stopping the hero from becoming like him if he doesn't want the new competition in his field.

✪ If the hero likes the Double character it may be hard for him to become like the Double. There will be no one left to look up to. The hero will then have to take responsibility for his own life and will have to live up to the man he idolizes.

The Double in action:

✪ Luke Skywalker wants to be just like his Father (the Double) in *Star Wars*. He idolizes him and has no idea his father is actually Darth Vader in the first film.

✪ Glinda the Good Witch is a Double and a guide in *The Wizard of Oz*. She possesses the strength, intelligence and goodness Dorothy is striving toward.

V The Feminine and Masculine Journeys

Chapter 23

Introduction to Archetypal Journeys

Now that you've been introduced to the character archetypes, this next section will take you through the stages of the feminine and masculine journeys. Once you develop your character and have an initial idea of the story you want to tell, you need to outline the story that your character will inhabit.

Each archetype will have a different approach to each step along the journey, whether it's a female hero on the masculine journey or a male hero on the feminine journey. The journeys aren't bound by gender, though more male characters tend to go down the masculine journey and vice versa.

Some characters will fight change every step of the way while others embrace it. Some characters choose to laugh at the world while others become distressed by it. It's up to you as the author to decide how your character will react in each stage of his journey. The archetype you have chosen for your character is a great guide for this.

A note on acts: In screenwriting, there is a three-act structure for a 120-page script where each page equals one minute of screen/time. Act I is the beginning and consists of the first thirty pages. Act II is the middle and consists of sixty pages. Act III is the end and consists of thirty pages. I use this act framework to help clarify the stages of the journeys.

For a quick overview:

❂ **The Feminine Journey** is a journey where a hero must

go deep inside herself and change throughout the story. This hero awakens in Act I and moves toward rebirth. Movies of the week and character-driven stories tend to fall into this category as well as *The Wizard of Oz*, *Titanic*, *American Beauty*, *Mother*, *The Awakening* and *Alien*.

This journey is based on the Descent of the goddess Inanna, one of the oldest recorded myths in history.

✪ **The Masculine Journey** is a journey where a hero resists inner change until Act III, where he must choose to awaken and find victory or choose to rebel against it and find failure. Traditional cop movies and action films tend to fall into this category as well as *Star Wars*, *The Long Kiss Goodnight*, *Lethal Weapon*, *Moby Dick*, *Three Kings* and *Dumb and Dumber*.

This journey is based on the ancient Mesopotamian myth, the Epic of Gilgamesh, from the seventh century B.C.

You can get really creative and find ways to add action and suspense to the feminine journey as *Alien* did, or to add strong character changes and growth to the masculine journey as *Three Kings* did.

The journeys are meant as guides for writers. They provide basic outlines to free you from worry about structure. Once you have the steps outlined you know where you're going. You can spend your time creating interesting characters and adding new twists to your story instead of thinking about the structure and direction of it. The journey stages are a tool to free your creativity. You can have one or one hundred pages in between the stages. It's totally up to you.

The following chapters discuss the feminine and masculine journeys. Each stage is outlined in detail with examples from popular films and classical literature. A section called "Gender Bending" shows a male hero on the feminine journey and a female hero on the masculine journey, and a craft tips section ends each stage to help get your creative juices flowing. But before we discuss the journeys in depth, we're going to look at the gender differences that inform each journey.

Gender Differences

While the journeys are different, each presents characters with chances to develop positive and negative traits. In *Diving Deep and Surfacing*, Carol P. Christ explains the differences: "Most psychologists (and writers) have tended to emphasize the positive aspects of the male model of development. In truth, both ways of developing produce different strengths and different weaknesses. If men's mode of developing gives them strong egos and a strong sense of self, it makes them less open to experiences of identification and sympathy, less likely to see other persons or other beings as like themselves, less open to mystical experiences. And if the negative side of women's development is that they have weaker egos than men, the positive side is that identification, sympathy, and mystical experiences are easier for them to achieve."

Understanding the main differences between the sexes allows male writers to create more authentic female characters and female writers to create more authentic male characters. For example, many female writers don't realize the pressure men live under to perform and provide for a family, while many male writers don't realize the fear of danger women have to confront in their daily lives. Having a female character walk down a dark alley at night without any worry tells female readers that either this character is a superhero afraid of nothing or the writer doesn't understand women at all.

The following three topics—power, support and perception of the world—are an overview of the different issues male and female characters face regardless of their archetype.

How a character internalizes these issues is up to you. A Father's Daughter may choose to ignore any injustices or inequalities women face because she wants to fit in with the men at work. She may face several instances of inequality where she has to use her defenses to deny what she sees. A King may have to surrender his power in order to survive but refuses to believe surrender could mean anything but defeat.

Differences in Power

Both men and women need to dissolve the ego to awaken. Women come into their power to realize their authentic goals and connectedness, whereas men let go of their power to realize their authentic goals and connectedness.

The female hero awakens at the end of Act I and travels down a path that leads her to her power, while the male hero travels down a path with his power intact and awakens at the beginning of Act III when he realizes his power holds him back from fully experiencing life. If he does not awaken he is on the path of destruction as Captain Ahab is in *Moby Dick*.

The awakening is like a form of surrender the character goes through, a rebirth into the unknown. It is a giving up of power and control for men and a gaining of it for women.

For a writer this can mean conveying a deep sense of responsibility, an inner transformation or a rethinking of the path chosen for a character. Even action stories about the tough and violent hero who must fight to save the girl sometimes end with the hero seen in a more sympathetic light. He looks back on all he's done and wishes he had done it differently; he becomes conscious. This is what elevates the story to one of a mythic journey rather than a plot of just "painting by numbers."

Many women realize they're living a life filled with other

people's goals and ambitions. They have no sense of what they truly want deep down inside until their world comes crashing down around them and they're forced to reexamine everything. Like Dorothy thrown into the Land of Oz, she's not in Kansas anymore, and she must learn to navigate her new world.

Many men realize the power they have in the world only helps them to reach the goals that society says are acceptable for them. For a man to say his goal is to stay home and raise children means he gives up some of his power because he isn't a "real" man according to what is deemed appropriate for men. The heroes in *Three Kings* give up their goal for the gold and decide to help the desperate people of the land. They realize their connection with others, and they surrender their power and their goal to save the people.

Differences in Support

Another major difference between the feminine and masculine journeys is one of support. The male hero is genuinely supported by the group and by society in general when he leaves to embark on his journey.

The female hero isn't genuinely supported in her effort to leave her community and embark on a journey. Think of the woman who leaves her husband and home to start a new life— Edna in Kate Chopin's *The Awakening* or the woman who picks up a gun because she wants to fight in a war in *G.I. Jane*.

When she tries to step out of the roles deemed acceptable for her she meets a societal force that seems overpowering. This sometimes is played out by people who attack her low self-esteem, convincing her that she can't possibly do what she would most love to do. Edna in *The Awakening* commits suicide under this pressure.

Not too many male heroes face such adversity when starting on their journey. Men are expected to go on a journey, to shoot for something better in life, to go out and grab their piece of the dream. A man may feel that he's depending on the woman to hold up the home front so he can embark on his journey. Sometimes a way for him to prove himself is by saving a woman.

Starting Out in Different Worlds

The Dangerous World for Women

Many women make plans around what is and is not safe to do, while other women choose to be blind to the dangers around them and often wind up in troublesome situations, like the Maiden. For some female characters, going out on a blind date is something they would never think of doing, let alone meeting a guy from a personal ad.

Fear can greatly inhibit a female character's life if she allows it to. The reader may also unconsciously judge her actions as well, thinking, "What was she doing there in the first place?" Blaming the victim seems to help people separate themselves from the crime. Think of Sarah Tobias (Jodie Foster) in *The Accused*.

This shows us why women loved *Thelma & Louise* so much. Two ordinary women, a housewife and a waitress, got to take back their power and overcome the fears all women face on a daily basis.

The Demanding World for Women

Women also must face the demands on them to have children and to be good housewives. Women are starting to expose the myth that tells them they can have it all—career, kids and marriage. Through exhaustion and stress, women are learning that they can't have it all.

Some are opting not to have children, which may make them feel ostracized on one hand and unwomanly on the other because womanhood and motherhood have always been seen as synonymous. Many will assume she is barren or just plain selfish when she tells them her decision. Your heroine may be working through these issues.

Women who choose to have children are realizing that they have to give up their careers for a few years in order to do it. This may make them feel like failures for not being able to do it all. Has your heroine given up career dreams to raise children?

The World of Expectations for Men
In this world of expectation men are bombarded with the "Three Ps" from society: Perform, Provide and Protect.

A man is told by the media and society that he must perform and perform well if he wants to be a real man. He must get the great career and money first and then he'll be worthy of a beautiful woman. Buy this car, get this job and wear these clothes and you'll have it made, he's told. You'll have to work night and day and will always be competing with other men to get it, but money is power and power is everything.

It might be devastating for a husband to later hear from his wife, "I wish you had more time to love me instead of your work." Is your hero confronted with this dilemma? He realizes he hasn't spent much time with the kids and has given up his real dreams because he couldn't make enough money doing them.

A man is also told that he must protect women and children, be strong and show no emotion. He must bare the burden of being responsible for anything that happens to his loved ones whether he could have helped or saved them if he was there or not. A man's life is seen as expendable—remember the men who couldn't get into the lifeboats on the Titanic. Is your hero afraid to expose his fears and to show himself as vulnerable?

✪

So what does all this mean? Only that there are some gender issues that writers need to be aware of. You may never once talk about any of these issues in your story but they may still find their way in through the subtext. Readers live these issues everyday, and they'll love and believe in a character who acts or reacts in tune with current gender issues. Think of how well *The First Wives Club* and *High Fidelity* did. These stories resonated with the male and female experience and audiences loved them.

Chapter 24

Plotting the Feminine Journey

The feminine journey is a journey in which the hero gathers the courage to face death and endure the transformation toward being reborn as a complete being in charge of her own life.

Her journey starts by questioning authority, then gaining the courage to stand up for herself and finally embodying the willingness to go it alone and face her own symbolic death. The nine-stage process is represented in three acts mirroring classic story structure.

The nine stages of her journey are:

Act I: Containment
1. The Illusion of a Perfect World
2. The Betrayal or Realization
3. The Awakening—Preparing for the Journey

Act II: Transformation
4. The Descent—Passing the Gates of Judgment
5. The Eye of the Storm
6. Death—All Is Lost

Act III: Emergence
7. Support
8. Rebirth—The Moment of Truth
9. Full Circle—Return to the Perfect World

ACT I

Stage 1: The Illusion of a Perfect World

A woman named Sarah sits staring through a window watching clouds glide freely across a perfect blue sky and tells herself, "Things are fine just the way they are."

Sarah has spent years building a perfect glass bubble around herself to shield her from the pain and uncertainty of taking risks for her own growth. Like "Sleeping Beauty," she is asleep to the real world around her and ignorant of the power she has to awaken herself. Sarah buys into the belief that if she plays by the rules she'll be rewarded for it. As time goes on the glass walls close in on her, closer and closer until she can't stand up anymore without hitting her head on the glass ceiling that has formed above her.

Rather than confront the glass ceiling that holds her down, the hero decides not to stand up. She uses her creativity to make do with her situation and avoid the truth that she lives in a world that works against her growth as a person.

She has a false sense of security about her future and thinks everyone will like her if she keeps it up. This is a safe world of things known to her; repetition brings her the illusion of security.

She may live naively in denial, hoping that others will take care of her, or she may play the martyr and accept her fate. She doesn't possess the motivation to explore an alternative option for herself.

She can't imagine risking everything to rescue herself from this world. She doesn't know there are better worlds out there to explore. "Doesn't everyone suffer?" she asks. She wants to make this world work so she can avoid the pain of change and growth.

What she cares about may be holding her in this place as well—supporting a family, waiting for that promotion, trying to save everyone else but herself or caring about what others think. These are just excuses to remain passive so she doesn't have to see the opportunities that surround her.

In order for the reader to believe the hero wouldn't be better off returning here when things get tough later on in the story, this world has to be set up as a negative place the hero can't function in. She may try hard to explain away the bad things that happen to her, but sooner or later she'll run out of excuses.

This "perfect world" must be shown as the negative place it is in order to motivate the hero to wake up. She must endure her quest for something better throughout the story because it's clear she can't function in her current world.

There are five coping strategies the hero may use to get by in the "perfect world." Through one of these five ways of dealing with the world the hero allows herself to remain blind to the reality of her situation. She learns how to fit in and establish herself using the traits her archetype has given her to her advantage.

The five coping strategies are:

○ **The Naive Strategy:** This woman has the view, conscious or otherwise, that "Other women may get hurt, attacked or passed over but not me. Nothing bad could ever happen to me. Life is good and I'll be rewarded for my efforts. I just have to wait it out."

For example:

In *The Wizard of Oz*, Dorothy lives in a black-and-white world where everything moves along at a steady pace. There's no color, no excitement, but plenty of repetition and comfort. She spends her time trying to find things to do. Life is boring to her and when she tries to help out with the chores, everyone tells her to go away. She seems out of place there. She doesn't realize she has a lot of growing up to do, and she'll need to get away from the farm to do it.

○ **The Cinderella Strategy:** This woman lives in a world where she relies on male protection and guidance to survive. "My man will always be there to support me and when I'm away from him other men will always come to my aid so I don't have to worry about anything bad happening to me. Men love to take care of me and treat me well." She may believe she has to be beautiful in order to hold on to men.

For example:

In *Gone With The Wind*, we first see Scarlett O'Hara sitting on her porch with two men doting on her. She continuously steers the conversation away from the war and onto herself in a very self-centered manner. She doesn't want to face reality outside of Tara, her estate. Her family's money brings her comfort and status. She refuses to see how she is kept in her place by the rules of this society that force women to take naps when they're not even tired. She's only concerned with attracting the attention of all the men she meets.

○ **The Exceptional Strategy:** This woman lives life in the boys' club, or so she thinks. She feels she is just as good as a man and is often told this by her peers. "Other women can't do this but I can because I'm the exception. Men appreciate me because I can act just like them and fit in their group. I never cry or complain." She can ignore any sexism she sees in the office because she doesn't identify herself as a "woman."

For example:

In *Working Girl*, Katherine Parker completely suppresses everything about herself that is feminine. She is always seen with "the boys," often making fun of the female secretaries in the office. She sees herself as the only woman who can do the job she does and is devastated when another woman—a mere secretary!—takes over. Tess McGill (Melanie Griffith) believes she's better than the other secretaries in the office; she couldn't take the chances she takes if she didn't feel this way. She separates herself from the other women completely so she can break into the boys' club.

○ **The Pleasing Strategy:** This woman lives to please others. As long as others are happy, she's happy. Her validation comes from others. She's like a compliant innocent girl who does everything by the book, suppressing her own female intuition and strength. Her actions support the status quo, and she rejects her true desires so she can fit in. This allows her to feel like she has control over her life; she won't be yelled at because she'll just do everything right. She walks on eggshells most of the time.

In *Thelma & Louise*, Thelma takes care of her domestic duties like she is supposed to, and she stays in a destructive marriage as is expected of her, but deep down she's unhappy. Even though her house is nice, clean and upper middle class, her world is self-destructive. We watch her tiptoe around her husband's verbally abusive behavior. She seems numb to most of what he says, and we realize this must have been going on for quite a long time.

○ **The Disappointed Type:** This type of woman is angry and depressed with her lot in life but doesn't act to change it—yet. She can be bitter and sarcastic, often the most outspoken woman in the office, or she can play the role of the martyr, sacrificing her welfare for others. Deep inside she dreams about her real goals, which seem so out of reach. She is the most aware of the five types and longs to find a positive female role model. She knows her world isn't perfect but doesn't have the desire or motive to change it.

In *Titanic*, Rose lives a very sheltered and controlled life.

At first we see her as a wealthy woman with a fiancé who loves her and servants to wait on her. Everything seems perfect but behind her eyes a hint of despair lurks. Slowly we learn her fiancé and her mother watch her every move. Everything is decided for her down to what she'll eat for dinner. We then realize she's playing the martyr to support her family and is doomed to live her life unhappy.

Examples of Stage 1

The Descent of Inanna translated by Wolkstein and Kramer

In the myths of the goddess Inanna, Inanna one day decides that she's ready for a throne and the wisdom that comes with it. She plants a tree and passively waits ten years for the tree to split open so she can make a throne for herself, but a snake (as the symbol of renewal), an anzu-bird (as the symbol of knowledge) and Lilith (the rebellious woman) have built their homes inside the trunk and the tree will not grow. (These three symbols are similar to the heart, brains and courage Dorothy seeks in *The Wizard of Oz*.)

In order to be worthy of the throne, Inanna must seize these three aspects of herself alone, but instead she calls on her brother Gilgamesh to get rid of them. He slays the creatures and builds the throne for her. His protection keeps her from embarking on her own journey, and she remains in her safe sheltered world.

The Wizard of Oz

As mentioned earlier Dorothy lives a simple life in a black-and-white world.

Titanic

As mentioned earlier, Rose lives a very sheltered and controlled life.

The Awakening by Kate Chopin

Edna is a martyr who's depressed with her lot in life. The story opens with her at a summer beach house visiting with her high society friends and trying to have fun despite her husband's mean disposition. She is close with Robert, a Woman's Man, who is the exact opposite of her husband. She has all the free time and money she could ever want as well as a husband and children. She is supposed to be happy, content and grateful, but a hint of despair lurks around her.

Gender-Bending: *American Beauty*

In the beginning of the film we see family pictures that tell us this is the perfect family. We see the family sitting together at perfect family meals, but we soon realize things are far from perfect. As Lester says, "I wish I could tell my daughter that all her anger, insecurity and confusion will pass but I don't want to lie to her."

Lester has lived his entire life pushing forty-plus hours in a job he hates. He turns around one day and realizes his entire life is a sham. Career accomplishments mean nothing if they're achieved according to someone else's view of what it means to be successful. He just took a job to have a job and climb a corporate ladder he wasn't sure he wanted to climb.

CRAFT TIPS FOR STAGE 1 OF THE FEMININE JOURNEY

✪ Come up with at least five different settings to show the "perfect world." If the office is where her perfect world is, think of all the different places she goes during her workday and pick the one that's the most creative.

- She may be found smoking a cigarette in the back alley of the office everyday at 9:03 A.M. to prepare herself to deal with a difficult boss. She may be the only doctor who visits with the janitors in the cafeteria to eat grape Jell-O every afternoon, and they may turn out to be her helpers later on.

○ Remember, you're introducing your hero to your reader in this stage and setting up the theme of the story.

○ Sometimes it helps to think about what happened to the character just before the opening scene to add some color to it or reveal more about the character. Did she have a hard time getting the children ready for school? Did her car break down? Did she win a raffle? Did she meet a great guy?

Stage 2: The Betrayal or Realization

As Sarah watches the sky from within her glass bubble, a huge cloud forms in front of her, blocking the bright sunlight.

Afraid of the dark, she backs away from the window. Lightning moves closer and closer. With one thunderous crash her bubble smashes wide open. Shards of glass fly everywhere around her.

The glass bubble smashes wide open, and all of life's juices spill on the floor. Everything important to the hero is taken away, and she is pushed to a fork in the road where she must make a choice between going out into the world to actively face her fears or staying where she is and becoming a passive victim. She is betrayed—by society, by herself or by a villain. This stage is also known as the inciting incident.

For character-driven stories that are pushed by the plot, like mysteries, use the elements of the mystery as a metaphor for her internal conflict. The mystery can bring her through all the stages as she tries to solve the case. Most likely her betrayal is more like a realization that she wants something more out of life, even if it is to just do the right thing for a change and solve the crime. This journey will still make her face her demons.

The betrayal has come so close to home the hero can't ignore it. It is staring her in the face, and she must deal with it. She realizes her life is different from what she thought it was, and there's no knight in shining armor to come to the rescue.

This stage sets the stakes and provides the hero with motivation to change her world. The system she has tried to work within doesn't reward her efforts like she expected. She's played the game by all the rules and has lost anyway; her world falls apart.

The hero asks herself, "What's the point? Why am I here? What's all this for?" She may have a nervous breakdown or succumb to addictions during this stage as she tries to reorganize her life. This stage gives the character motivation that carries the whole story to completion. It must be strong. She can't just undo or easily forget what has happened to her here.

This is where the coping strategy the character has chosen falls apart. It no longer works for her, and her whole life and everything she believes in has changed. A role may be over for her (motherhood, for example), and she can't go back in time to change it.

○ The Naive Strategy: This woman is hurt or abused. A close friend or family member who took care of her dies. A major crisis turns her world upside down. She loses her job or house or money.

In *The Wizard of Oz*, Dorothy feels betrayed by her uncle when he doesn't protect Toto from the nasty neighbor who wants to put him to sleep. She feels all alone. In fact, her parents aren't there at all; they have betrayed her by dying and leaving her alone.

○ The Cinderella Strategy: This woman is left without

male protection or support. The man may have died.

In *Gone With the Wind*, Scarlett is betrayed by the men who leave her to fight in the war and to nurse the sick. She is also betrayed by her beloved Ashley, who marries another woman.

○ **The Exceptional Strategy:** This woman is passed over for a promotion or otherwise betrayed by her male peers proving she isn't as good as a man or one of the boys. She can't get into the men's club. She loses a big contract. She loses her marriage because she can't juggle career and marriage. If she's involved with the church, she may lose faith in God as she learns she isn't allowed to become a priest, leading her to question her whole religion.

In *Working Girl*, Tess McGill is betrayed by her boyfriend when she comes home to find him in bed with another woman. She's also betrayed by Katherine Parker when she puts her name on Tess's report, taking the credit for her work.

○ **The Pleasing Type:** This woman finds herself trampled on; people take advantage of her. Some may even put her down as being "only" a mother, secretary, assistant, etc. She feels totally devalued. She may even be penalized for taking time off to have a child.

In *Thelma & Louise*, Thelma is betrayed first by a husband who is mean and nasty to her, then later by a man who tries to rape her. She was just being nice and polite and never saw the danger she was getting into.

○ **The Disappointed Type:** This woman is pushed too far, usually by another person in a position of power. She may feel backed up against a wall, unable to move in any direction to avoid the attack or humiliation that's coming.

In *Titanic*, Rose is betrayed by her father because he squandered away the family's money and died leaving them penniless. Then her mother betrays her by forcing her into an engagement with an abusive man she doesn't love. It's clear she's been doing what she's told for a very long time. When her fiancé beats her she decides to kill herself. The whole world has betrayed her; womanhood has betrayed her as well because as a woman she doesn't think she'll ever be able to ride horses and explore the world like she dreams of doing.

✪

If your character is facing an internal "What's my life all about?" then she'll willingly move toward transformation and face villains in the form of people telling her she's not capable to go on the journey. We'll discuss this in the next stage.

This is the stage where the villain is set up. Make sure the villain, the one who betrays, has a good reason for doing what he is doing.

Think of how memorable the villain Hannibal Lecter is in *The Silence of the Lambs*. He isn't shown as just some insane man but is given moments of extreme mental clarity and professionalism that make him almost endearing.

Villains never believe themselves to be bad or wrong. They have concrete reasons behind what they do and truly believe they're right and everyone else is wrong.

Rose's fiancé in *Titanic* believes that he truly loves her and that she is blessed to be with him. He even gives her the most expensive necklace in the world to prove it. He feels he has gone out of his way to please her. He believes he does everything for her and that she is simply ungrateful.

Examples of Stage 2

The Descent of Inanna translated by Wolkstein and Kramer

One of Inanna's betrayals comes from the god of wisdom. One day Inanna pays him a visit and "with youthful audacity, she boasts that *she* will bless him. But he refers to her as *the young woman*, and bids his servant to treat her *as if she were equal with him*."

After an afternoon of drinking and feasting he laughingly gives all of his holy possessions to her. She accepts his gifts and joyfully leaves with them. When he sobers up he is outraged that his possessions are gone. He sends his servant to get the gifts back from Inanna. Inanna is crushed when she hears this news. "She sees him as a tyrant, a fraud, a monstrous liar."

Depressed and devastated, she realizes that all the dogs in the land have homes but she, the queen, has nowhere to call home. Enlil the sky god has made her a wanderer. "He has filled me, the queen of heaven, with consternation . . . the dog kneels at the threshold, but I—I have no threshold."

Gilgamesh also turns against her, insulting her in order to steal her power.

She is courted by Dumuzi, the Shepard King of Uruk, but she states several times that she doesn't love him and wants to marry a farmer instead. Her mother and brother convince her to do otherwise.

The Wizard of Oz
As mentioned earlier, Dorothy feels betrayed by both her uncle when he doesn't protect Toto from the nasty neighbor who wants to put him to sleep, and her parents because they aren't there for her.

Titanic
As mentioned earlier, Rose is betrayed by her father because he squandered away the family's money, and by her mother planning an arranged marriage for her.

The Awakening by Kate Chopin

Edna's husband is out late playing billiards. He never pays much attention to her when he's in town. He comes home and gets upset. For no reason he scolds her for not being motherly enough to their children. She is betrayed by a husband who wants to control her every move, a society that expects her to be content with motherhood as her role and by other women who play that role perfectly, making her look like an outcast.

Gender-Bending: *American Beauty*

At work Lester is a pleaser. He obviously hates his job but he smiles and goes with the flow in order to keep it. He is called into the new boss's office and told that he must write down why he is valuable to the company so they can decide if they'll fire him or not. He's worked there for fourteen years and is outraged that they would do this to him. He feels unwanted, unappreciated and useless. When he goes home that night, we see he feels that way with his family, too. He takes a passive role; he never even drives the car.

CRAFT TIPS FOR STAGE 2 OF THE FEMININE JOURNEY

❂ By the end of this betrayal readers should be asking themselves, "What will she do now?"

❂ To help build the suspense, believability and drama of the betrayal ask these questions:

* Can you add another character, a family member perhaps, to build the suspense?
* Have you set up the villain enough so his actions are believable?
* Can you change the setting, time or even the hero's archetype to make it more dramatic?

❂ Make sure the villain has a great reason for doing what

he's doing to the hero.

❂ Think about other supporting characters you can add to set up even more conflict.

❂ Comedies like those of Albert Brooks use this stage with great effect. His character is passed over for a promotion in *Lost in America*, he loses his wife in *Mother*, and he loses his career and creativity in *The Muse*.

Stage 3: The Awakening—Preparing for the Journey

Suddenly someone appears offering to help Sarah rebuild her glass bubble, but at a very high price. As she considers her options she notices a rough jagged path leading the way out of the rubble. As she breathes the fresh air for the first time she realizes it's not worth spending what little she has left to rebuild it.

Stretching her neck she tries to see where the path goes but it just disappears into the horizon. She decides to take a chance and venture forth anyway. Several people try to talk her out of it, pointing out how sharp the pieces of broken glass are along the way.

Not being able to see where the path leads, Sarah gathers tools she thinks will help her on the journey. As she says good-bye to those around her, she makes an ally. Whether she realizes it or not, she has friends who support her.

The hero has been betrayed or has come to a harsh realization about her life. What will she do now? Hopelessness and helplessness tempt her into depression, rage and bitterness. She can take the passive road and:

- Blame others.
- Blame herself.
- Be a victim and ask, "Why me?"
- Avoid the situation by absorbing herself in busyness.
- Decide to commit suicide like Rose in *Titanic*.

On the other hand, she can take the active road where she sees the betrayal as:

- A lesson.
- An invitation to freedom and change.
- A challenge to go after what she wants.

She may first respond to the betrayal in a passive way or she may rage for all the time she has lost, but soon she decides to do something about it.

If she is lost in the passive response, another character can bring her back on track, but it's her decision to act that creates a turning point, sets up the main goal, moves the story forward and changes the hero's life forever. She has decided to say "yes" to what she wants, and most importantly to say "no" to what she doesn't want.

This is when many other characters come out of the woodwork to tell her she can't accomplish the goal, she needs help or that she's crazy. In some cases it's her own inner critic trying to sabotage her. But the force of the betrayal she suffered pushes her to overcome this negativity.

If she's lucky another character will be supportive and push the hero along, asking, "Why do you let them treat you like that?" But don't bring a hero along to save the day for her or she'll never get to embark on her own journey.

She may:

- Give up the superwoman mystique and refuse to take care of everyone at home and on the job.
- Speak the truth to a loved one regardless of the consequences.
- Ask for that raise she's always wanted or ask to work on a special project.
- Set new boundaries.
- Start a business or leave one.
- Agree to testify against someone.
- Decide to go after the killer.

- Travel across the country to find herself.
- Ask questions when she's told to be silent.
- Decide to fight for her beliefs.
- Insist she saw what she saw even if it was a UFO or a ghost. Her female intuition won't be suppressed.

Whatever it is, this decision changes her life and pushes her toward a concrete goal. This stage is a reversal of sorts. The whole direction of the hero's life will be forever changed by her decision in this stage of the game.

The End of the Coping Strategy

At this stage, whatever coping strategy she used to get along in the "perfect world" is useless to her now. She abandons it in order to fully move into her archetype and all its attributes. The coping strategy is what kept her from seeing the betrayal. She steps into her archetype using its assets to her advantage.

Think of Thelma in *Thelma & Louise*. She awakens and decides to keep going with Louise. For the first time she doesn't care what her husband will say or what the consequences of her actions are. She has freedom in her sight.

Preparing for the Journey

Another part of this stage is the preparation for the journey.

Not being able to see where the path leads, the hero gathers tools she thinks will help her on the journey. As she says good-bye to those around her, she makes an ally whether she realizes it or not. In her mind she has a list of people she thinks will help her if she needs help.

Like Little Red Riding Hood who gathers her basket, the hero finds the tools she thinks she'll need to survive. The problem is that she's still looking for things outside of herself to help her.

Her preparation can include:

❂ Saying her good-byes.

❂ Asking others their opinions on what she should do.

❂ Gathering weapons—guns, money, disguises.

❂ Documenting all the wrongs that have been done to her, as victims of sexual harassment or those being stalked must do.

❂ Gathering clothing and other items she thinks she needs to be seen as beautiful or professional as the women in *Working Girl* do.

If she's an activist she may gather tools to chain herself to a tree she wants to save or create signs that make strong statements. If she's battling the corporate establishment she may make copies of files and data. If she's a mother running away from an abusive husband she'll gather her children, clothing and money before she leaves.

Armed with these weapons the hero feels safer but there's nothing in that basket that can save Little Red Riding Hood from the jaws of the Big Bad Wolf. Essentially it's her courage and smarts that will help her, but she doesn't really trust herself yet.

A mentor may show up but often doesn't have all the information the hero needs because her journey is one where she goes more into herself to find her own strength rather than relying on others.

All the ogres and tyrants step into the forefront:

❂ Self-doubt creeps over her; she thinks, "Maybe they're right, I can't do this."

❂ She's told she's not smart or prepared enough and wastes time trying to get information she doesn't need.

❂ The male hero comes to save the day for her. Men are told to help and save women as part of their journey as heroes but in doing so women are kept from embarking on their own journeys.

⊘ There's also the "man who would understand" as author Adrienne Rich calls him. This man pretends to understand what she's going through, but then stops supporting her. He seemed sympathetic to her cause before her awakening and now deserts her when the going gets tough.

⊘ The rules are changed:

- All of a sudden her job will have more work for her to do, pulling her out of her journey.
- School will change policies on her, making it harder to get her degree.
- Sneaky liars dangle golden carrots just out of her reach telling her, "Go on, waste your time reaching for it."
- The Motor Vehicle Bureau decides to give out her new address to a stalker.

⊘ Her fear of hurting others may overcome her.

⊘ Her inability to say "no" gets her in trouble as she stops to help someone.

⊘ She gets wrapped up in other people's dramas.

Examples of Stage 3

The Descent of Inanna translated by Wolkstein and Kramer

In Inanna's case she realizes she must stop crying over things others are doing to her and take control herself. She must journey to the underworld and face herself. "To prepare for her journey, Inanna gathers together the seven Me (attributes of civilization which also correspond to the seven chakras; see the seven issues of Stage 4) . . . she transforms them into such feminine allure as a crown, jewelry and a gown to wear as her protections. In case she would not return from the underworld, Inanna instructs her friend Ninshubur to remind her 'fathers' of her."

The Wizard Of Oz

Dorothy awakens when she opens the door to her house and sees the bright land of Oz. It's as if her eyes are open for the first time. She is also left alone to go on this journey without her family. They've been too protective of her.

Titanic

The awakening comes for Rose when, after being beaten by the fiancé her mother wants her to marry, she watches a little girl in a frilly white dress at a table near her, who is a mirror character of Rose. This little girl is being told to sit up straight and to hold her napkin properly. The girl is being robbed of her childhood, and Rose is being robbed of her womanhood.

She realizes she'll never be able to grow into the fun-loving woman she wants so desperately to be. Rose changes her mind and decides to meet Jack, a lower-class artist she's been forbidden to see. She tells him that she trusts him as he holds to the front of the ship with her arms outstretched, and she poses in the nude as a model for one of his portraits. She breaks out of her shell.

The Awakening by Kate Chopin

Edna goes to swim in the ocean with Robert even though it may not be the proper thing to do. The sensuous waves enfold her body and she begins to realize that she is *a person with a place in the world*. She confides in Madam Ratignolle, trying to find a female friend as she prepares to change, but it doesn't work out well.

Mademoiselle Reisz comes along as a mentor to her but

she brings warnings that if Edna wishes to flaunt convention she'll have to endure isolation like she has.

Gender-Bending: *American Beauty*
Lester overhears his daughter and her girlfriend talking about him. He rushes into the garage, finds his dumbbells and takes off his clothes. Stripped naked, he examines himself and starts to workout. He takes the first step toward changing his life.

CRAFT TIPS FOR STAGE 3 OF THE FEMININE JOURNEY

✪ Create several different types of supporting characters to cut down her decision. Sometimes being laughed at by the one closest to us is the most devastating. Who does she look up to?

✪ Remember to show the hero's awakening instead of telling it. Let her actively show the decision she has made. Does her boss constantly ask her to get him coffee when she's a vice president? Perhaps she dumps it in his lap and walks out. Think of how drastically different and alive the world of Oz is as compared to Kansas.

✪ This is where the hero abandons her coping strategy.

✪ All major supporting characters should have all been introduced to the reader by now, whether the hero has met them or not.

ACT II
Stage 4: The Descent—Passing the Gates of Judgment

Sarah is a little uneasy being outside her bubble but she notices the air is much cleaner. She grasps her weapons and stands at the gates of the underworld. She has faced the fear that held her back and said no to the liars and tyrants that tried to stop her.

> She steps through the gate, descends the staircase and sees there are six more gates waiting for her. It's too late for her to turn around now. At each succeeding gate a gatekeeper steps out and strips her of one of her weapons until she is left naked and alone in the darkness.

Now that the hero has made a life-changing decision she has to face the changes that come with it. She may also have to face societal assumptions that women are weak, passive and powerless as she tries to move forward.

The hero faces one of her fears, an obstacle that has much more at stake than mere self-doubt. She may want to turn back on her journey. She tries to use her weapons—manipulation, blackmail, her sexuality, her troubled past and wounds—but they don't work. One by one she passes the gates of judgment, faces a fear and loses a weapon in the process. She is stripped of all the external devices she thought would save her.

Keep in mind that what the hero faces in this stage is only a precursor to what she'll face in Stage 6, Death. In this stage Dorothy in *The Wizard of Oz* feels guilty about leaving home when her family needs her, but in Stage 6 she faces the guilt that her leaving home will literally kill her Aunt. The stakes are raised much higher in Stage 6.

In the *Descent of Inanna*, Inanna passes through seven gates, losing one of her adornments or a part of her queenly identity at each one. These seven gates are compared to the seven chakras of the body and the seven demons cast out of people on a spiritual path as well as the seven primary colors of the rainbow.

These seven issues can be used to help you flesh out the plot points of your hero's descent in this stage. All of the archetypes can face these issues on their journeys. It's purely up to you which ones she'll face and how they'll become part of the plot.

✪ **Issue of Facing Fear, Surviving and Finding Safety and Security:** Is the hero afraid of intimacy because of fear of abandonment? Is she afraid to depend on someone else? Does she push herself too much? Is she able to support herself and put a roof over her head? What fear is she avoiding?

✪ **Issues of Facing Guilt, Expressing Sexuality and Emotions and Knowing One's Desires:** Does the hero want to say "no" but can't out of fear of rejection? Does she prefer to remain distant from others? Does she have a hard time setting limits because she doesn't want others to get mad? Does she sabotage her relationships? Does she know what makes her feel good? What does she feel guilty about?

✪ **Issues of Facing Shame, Defining Power and Will, and Gaining Her Own Identity:** Is the hero highly critical of herself? Is she a perfectionist? Does she want power over or power with others? Does she exercise her willpower? Does she try to control everything? How does she feel about money? Does she overindulge and binge? Does she have a sense of herself, or is she in an identity crisis? Why does she feel shame? Do others intentionally shame her?

✪ **Issues of Facing Grief, Giving and Receiving Love, Being in Relationships and Accepting Herself:** Does the hero feel like she doesn't fit in? Is she self-conscious in social situations? Does she need to have someone else tell her what the right thing to do is? How does she behave toward others? Can she have a lasting relationship without sabotaging it? Does she accept herself as she is? What is she grieving over?

✪ **Issues of Facing Lies and Communicating and Expressing Herself:** Can she speak her mind? Is she afraid to stand out? Is she rebellious and overactive? Has she bought into all the negative statements others make about her? What lies has she told herself? What lies has someone else told her? Is she confused? Does she suppress her creativity?

۞ Issues of Facing Illusion, Honoring Intuition and Imagination: Is the hero afraid to find out who she is and see things clearly? Is she in denial? Does she have a lack of imagination? Does she ignore her gut feelings and intuition? Does she feel worthy of the positive side of her archetype? What illusion does she buy into?

۞ Issues of Facing Attachment and Finding Self-Awareness: Is the hero open-minded? Or does she blindly obey others? Does her inner critic sabotage her ability to succeed and be responsible? Does she allow life to teach her? Does she learn from her mistakes? Is she able to understand what's happening to her and see the outcome of her actions? Is she aware of her own motives? Is she too attached to her family or job to be able to know herself?

Ultimately the hero must give up all control and completely surrender herself and all of her weapons on the descent. Stripped of all her coping mechanisms she must confront her demons. If shame is an issue for her she'll be shamed so she can face and later heal it. If survival is an issue for her she'll lose her means of support so she can support herself later on.

Think of Dorothy in *The Wizard of Oz*—home and family are the most important things to her; they mean survival. She finds herself all alone in the Land of Oz, her home and family gone. While the plot is about her finding her way home, the descent is about her facing her fears, facing the guilt of leaving her Aunt, facing illusions in the forest as well as in Oz and making new friends and forming relationships.

This hero must give up the path of resistance used by those on the masculine path, the path that fights against the flow of things, and instead move into the path of allowance, going with the flow of events and taking each one in stride. Brains and courage are what she needs to find now—like Dorothy who finds the Scarecrow "brains" and the Lion "courage." Later when she ascends she will learn to have the "heart" of the Tin Man which will allow her to temper her courage and brains with compassion.

She must also learn to trust her instincts, which tell her not to trust a certain person or situation, or she'll be pulled down the wrong path, opening doors that lead nowhere.

For the first time she comes face-to-face with the villain or his goons and barely survives. She is cut down. She doesn't think she can last one more minute. This isn't what she bargained for.

She reminiscences even if just for a moment that things were much easier before. She may even want to go back to the old world, the safe world. That's why it must be shown to be a bad place for her. The betrayal (or realization) must be strong enough to carry her through this. She will long for the comfort of the familiar and to make the best of what she had. She'll be tempted to settle for something less than what she truly wants.

Examples:

✪ If she quit her job, she may be unable to find another one, and the bills are piling up around her. She is evicted from her home. (Survival)

✪ If her husband left her, she is feeling totally alone and depressed. He may try to come back into her life just as her date cancels. (Rejection and Loneliness)

✪ She may be forced to confront the one who verbally or physically attacked her. (Power)

✪ She may have to face being humiliated and vulnerable in order to save someone or something. (Shame)

✪ She may have to give up everything she owns and everything she knows and flee. She may have to venture off into a new town or country to hide. (Attachment)

✪ She may have an experience that makes her feel different from everyone else, possibly a mystical or psychic experience. (Illusion and Intuition)

✪ She may have found where the killer lives but arrives only in time to watch the next victim die. She has failed terribly, but searches for a clue. (Guilt)

She's like Little Red Hiding Hood with a basket that holds nothing of use to her against the Big Bad Wolf. Only brains and courage give her the strength to continue on to Grandma's house unharmed.

This stage is often seen in horror films with female protagonists. The woman meets the killer and begins her descent into hell as the killer stalks her. Think of Laurie Strode (Jamie Lee Curtis) in *Halloween*. Alone with nothing but the clothes on her back, she must try to survive the ordeal.

Examples of Stage 4

The Descent of Inanna translated by Wolkstein and Kramer
Inanna descends and is judged at each of the seven gates where she is disrobed and humiliated. Each garment taken from her was worn over one of her chakra centers. (See the previous seven issues faced.)

All of her seven Me (attributes of civilization) are taken from her and she is left naked in front of the dark goddess Ereshkigal. All of her old illusions, false identities and defenses count for nothing in the underworld. She says she wanted to gain power and knowledge over death by witnessing another's funeral rites rather than by experiencing it herself ". . . but to enter the underworld can bring Inanna the possibility of being witness to only one funeral, her own."

The Wizard of Oz

Dorothy is given the ruby slippers to help her on her journey. She ventures into the forest and meets several helpers along the way.

They come upon the Wicked Witch of the West who tries to burn the Scarecrow. Dorothy tells her, "I don't want any trouble, we've come a long way already!" and the Witch replies, "You call that long? You've only just begun." They then descend into the dark forest of creepy wild animals.

Titanic

Rose and Jack descend through the bowels of the ship as her fiancé's goon chases them. They hide and she seduces him. Jack is falsely arrested. Rose refuses to get on a lifeboat and risks her life to save Jack.

The Awakening by Kate Chopin

Mademoiselle Reisz plays the piano and it unleashes Edna's painful emotions. She swims in the ocean again and goes out too far and panics. She tells her husband but he says he was watching her the whole time.

Something has changed inside her and she decides to test the waters of their marriage. When her husband orders her inside for the night, she disobeys him and he turns it around on her by staying outside longer than she can handle so she has to go in first. She tries to crush her wedding ring, she refuses to go on a business trip with him, she refuses to see callers and keep up with their social life and she decides to spend all of her time painting. Her husband goes to the doctor to find out why she's suddenly talking about equal rights.

Gender-Bending: *American Beauty*

Lester Burnham descends when he tells his wife, "This hasn't been a marriage for years but you were happy as long as I kept my mouth shut . . . I've changed." He goes jogging and smokes pot, and his wife tries to stop him.

Lester quits his job and blackmails the boss. He comes home and shouts at the dinner table and throws food around. He buys a Pontiac Firebird because it's what he always wanted. He's trying to find himself.

CRAFT TIPS FOR STAGE 4 OF THE FEMININE JOURNEY

✪ Remember to raise the stakes of her inner conflict here as well as her outer conflict. What assets would her archetype use? What flaws would she fall back on?

✪ Since this stage is driven by inner conflict, find five ways to externalize the character's feelings. Very often people facing the death of a loved one will come home and clean out their cabinets as if they're trying to clean out their lives and their emotions. So think about externalizing feelings.

✪ Remember this is the stage where her fears will be used against her.

✪ Come up with several fears for her to face, keeping in mind that Stage 6, Death, is where she'll face her biggest fear.

✪ This stage ends with a mini climax.

Stage 5: The Eye of the Storm

Sarah collapses on the basement floor. She listens for a sound in the darkness, but all is quiet. She breathes a sigh of relief and relaxes her muscles a bit. She thinks back and realizes she didn't step on any of the sharp pieces of glass from her broken bubble. She is unharmed and OK.

In the distance she sees a light. She thinks it leads to the other side and that her journey is completed. That is until footsteps approach.

After facing her fears and possibly the villain as well, the hero comes to terms with what just happened, and she feels she handled everything well. She gains a false sense of security. Somehow she stuck things out. She thinks this is the end of her journey and takes it easy for a moment.

She won't be getting off that easy, however. She still has to step up to the plate and actively reach for her goal; facing the problem isn't enough. For now she licks her wounds and pats herself on the back, eager to return home and tell everyone what has happened.

She gets a small taste of success, however false, which will later fuel her motive to succeed again, knowing how wonderful success feels. She feels safe for the time being. Sometimes the reader is given clues that the journey isn't over yet, especially if the book is barely half over!

Examples:

- She's told not to testify and she'll be safe.
- She spends time with her lover and feels OK again.
- She accomplishes something she has been trying to do for a long time and may try to substitute it for her real goal.
- Maybe her husband returns home and he's an easy way out of her loneliness.
- Her abuser is arrested.
- She's told she'll get promoted after all.
- She's told not to worry her pretty little head because it's all over now.
- She's told she really is valued and was just imagining things.

Often this false sense of security is conveyed in a montage or scene sequence showing happiness and hope.

The hero relaxes a bit and possibly takes a chance she shouldn't take. The villain watches from afar laughing, scheming and waiting.

Supporting characters want to take her home. They're afraid if she breaks out of the mold they're all in, what will become of them. Their world will have to change, too, if she's successful. "What will become of us if she is able to leave?" they think. "We'll have no excuses left of our own to stay in our own perfect worlds."

She may meet someone else who seems worse off then her. She may help this person thinking the reason she's here is to help others. She doesn't have to go through it, but soon she'll realize the only way out is through her own pain.

Examples of Stage 5

The Descent of Inanna translated by Wolkstein and Kramer
Inanna meets Ereshkigal, the dark goddess, and cries with her, sharing her tears as part of the funeral rites she came to witness. She thinks she's successful that Ereshkigal welcomes her and since she is the only one ever to meet Ereshkigal in person and survive. She feels safe.

The Wizard of Oz
Dorothy stepped into the light, made it through the poisoned poppy field and now stands at the gate of Oz—they made it! They're granted entrance and are treated like royal guests.

Titanic
Rose gets on a lifeboat, thinking Jack will be able to get on his own boat after her. It seems as if they'll both survive this ordeal, but she has her doubts.

The Awakening by Kate Chopin

Edna's husband leaves on a business trip and sends the kids to their grandparents' house. Edna is alone, quiet and content. She makes new friends and does new things. She wins money at the races and meets a new man named Arobin.

She decides to move into a smaller house by herself. She wants to be self-sufficient, no longer her husband's possession.

Gender-Bending: *American Beauty*

Lester seems happy for the first time in his life. He jogs and is in shape. He gets a chance to sleep with the young girl he fantasizes about but he makes the honorable decision to turn her down. He seems to have gotten his act together.

CRAFT TIPS FOR STAGE 5 OF THE FEMININE JOURNEY

✪ Come up with different ways for her to feel safe, to gain that false sense of security.

✪ This is the best stage to use some suspense. The hero feels safe, but the reader doesn't have to believe she's safe.

✪ Try a foreshadowing device to hint that things will be falling apart again soon.

✪ The villain can seem defeated at this point, but give him a way out.

✪ Like Innana, she can think she's there to help someone else through his pain, not realizing the only way out now is through her own pain and she won't have anyone there to hold her hand.

Stage 6: Death—All Is Lost

Sarah hears the footsteps coming closer and closer. All her weapons are gone. She backs herself into a corner and curls up as a large figure approaches, taunting her.

The air smells putrid, the dirt muddy. Why did she come here? There's no hope now. "I give up. I can't do this." She lies on her side and closes her eyes. She doesn't have any strength left to fight.

All of a sudden the villain comes back and everything does an about-face. She thought it was all over, that she could go back to her life a new person, but now things are starting all over again. This stage is like a reversal, and it ends with a dark moment where all seems lost. The villain can still be societal— a woman pushed down is expected to remain down so others can feel good about rescuing her. She isn't supported when she tries to stand on her own.

The villain isn't laughing anymore. He feels threatened by her accomplishments and means to destroy her. He sees that her inner turmoil is doing half of the job for him. All he needs to do is give her a push, cut her down and strengthen her weaknesses. He throws an additional betrayal at her or causes her to feel stupid like a nonperson.

She is captured, humiliated, tossed around and left to die. It's over. She failed at her journey and accepts defeat. She wanders confused about the turn of events and can't understand where everything went wrong. She can't see the gifts that await her on the other side.

❂ If her husband left her, this is when she sees him with the other woman and loses something else at the same time— a job, house, money.

❂ If she was attacked, this is when she faces her attacker and the stakes are raised to where he's set free.

❂ If she was passed over at work, this is when the promotion has been given to someone else. They fabricate information in her file to make her look bad so they can fire her.

✪ She finds herself not only trampled on but also humiliated, all her resources cut off from her.

✪ She is betrayed again.

✪ She may face a literal death experience.

Stage 4, the Descent, showed more of her inner conflict and turmoil. This stage shows her outer plot-driven conflict with the villain. Little Red Riding Hood faced the wolf in the forest, and she now must face the fact that he ate her grandmother and is waiting to eat her, too.

This is a great place to add a supporting character to make the situation even worse for the hero.

Many novels with female protagonists end here, especially those of Virginia Woolf and Edith Wharton. The hero of their time tried to flaunt convention and go against society but was so unsupported she could never make it successfully out of this stage. There was no one to come to her aid or to agree with her. She either chose death, was ostracized or went back to her old life a martyr.

In *The Deep End of the Ocean* by Jacquelyn Mitchard, the hero descends when she obsesses about finding her lost son. In the death stage she sleeps away in her depression, having given up on everything in life. She is lost in a "dark night of the soul" experience.

Examples of Stage 6

The Descent of Inanna translated by Wolkstein and Kramer

Inanna stands face to face with the dark goddess Ereshkigal. "The all-seeing judges at the gates of the underworld perceive Inanna's hidden, split-off parts and condemn her. Ereshkigal cries out, 'Guilty!' and Inanna is killed." She hangs on a peg to rot.

The Wizard of Oz

The Wizard demands that Dorothy bring him the witch's broom or he won't grant their wishes. This is another betrayal for her and a reversal in the story. On her journey to find the broom Dorothy is kidnapped and sentenced to die by the Wicked Witch of the West.

Titanic

Rose jumps off the lifeboat and races toward Jack. They kiss. He asks her why she did it and she replies, "You jump, I jump, remember?" He is all she cares about and she'll risk everything to be with him. She can face death with him at her side. The rest of the film is about them caught in the death stage waiting for the ship to sink.

The Awakening by Kate Chopin

Edna rushes to her friend's house to help her give birth. The violent pain her friend must endure terrifies her. When she starts to leave, her friend tells Edna she knows about Edna's affair with Arobin and that she should "remember the children!"

Edna feels that "her children threaten to chain her to a life of misery." When she returns to her new home she finds Robert, the love of her life, has left her for good. He's unable to face the ridicule that would come if she left her husband for him.

Edna stands naked on the beach for a moment. The only one who supports her is a woman who warns her of the isolation that comes with flaunting convention. Edna walks into the water and swims to her death.

Gender-Bending: *American Beauty*

Lester sits admiring a picture of his family and gets shot in the head by a man who is terrified to go on his own journey of self-exploration. There's no room in society for the man who wants to flaunt convention either.

CRAFT TIPS FOR STAGE 6 OF THE FEMININE JOURNEY

✪ Stretch your imagination as to how one would react in different situations. Use the character archetypes. Don't fall for stereotypes. Not all women will fall into depression when their husbands leave; some will avoid it by going out and having one-night stands, while others may buy a gun or go back to school.

✪ Watch some *Seinfeld* episodes to see how the actions of a supporting character in the beginning of a story come back to ruin all the plans of the main character by the end of the story. This show is a master of it! Can a supporting character make this stage even worse?

Act III
Stage 7: Support

Sarah lies on the cold damp floor, her eyes and ears shut. She can't find her way out. Not one drop of light shines, and she can't tell which way is left and which is right.

A voice calls to her, and she lifts her head. In the distance a match illuminates an ascending staircase. It was there the whole time, but she couldn't find it. She picks herself up and follows the light. She thinks, "I thought I was all alone here."

The female journey includes the relation between the individual and the group. The hero goes through her own awakening and comes out willing to accept help from others. She can't be betrayed again because she has her own strength and self-realization that can't be taken away from her. She is like the prisoner who finds freedom of spirit within her jail cell. It doesn't matter what anyone tries to do to her or take away from her.

She accepts others as they are and embraces the female aspect of supporting one another. She begins to see the oneness that we all share together.

Many a woman who has raised children feels anguish at not having a large community of women to help her out. Having become such isolated family units, the days are gone when she could ask a neighbor to watch her kids on the spur of the moment. There's strength in numbers, and the hero realizes it's OK to be in a group even if it's only with one other person who understands her.

In some cases, like mysteries and horror stories, the hero finds herself totally alone as everyone else has died or disappeared. In this case another character has already set up the tools or set out the information she'll need to find her way out. She's still being helped.

In other cases she's still alone but she seems to draw strength from her beliefs or allows a "spirit" to guide her, as with Joan of Arc.

While the masculine hero may need to do things totally on his own to prove himself to the group, the feminine hero needs to prove herself to herself and then share this knowledge with the group. She accepts that she is female and embraces it as a positive thing. So often she has tried to become a man to live in a man's world. Now she'll define her own world.

The hero lets someone else lend her a hand, give her a boost, and in turn that person will be exposed to the benefits of going on an inner journey. Her journey affects and guides others, so this isn't a handout she's receiving but an example she's giving. Very often supporting characters have problems of their own to overcome, and the hero can allow them to make amends through helping her.

Examples of Stage 7

The Descent of Inanna translated by Wolkstein and Kramer
After three days Inanna's friend Ninshubur pleads Inanna's case before her fathers. None of them will lend her support except Enki, her mother's father. He's the only one who values the path of descent and sends forth two androgynous beings to go to the underworld and mourn with Ereshkigal, to show her compassion. She restores Inanna to life but "no one ascends from the underworld unmarked. If Inanna wishes to return she must provide someone in her place."

The Wizard of Oz
Dorothy is captured by the Wicked Witch of the West and left to die. Her friends, the Scarecrow, the Tin Man and the Cowardly Lion come to her rescue, and through it they find heart, courage and brains of their own. She has friends who support and care about her. They'll sacrifice their own safety to help her.

Titanic
Rose has Jack, a Double (symbol character) of her own active and ambitious desires. He encourages her and guides her but admits that "the only one who can save Rose is Rose." He doesn't do it for her but provides her with the space, knowledge and example she needs in order to change. He helps her throughout the entire film as she descends and literally faces death. He then makes her promise she'll survive and do all the things they talked of doing.

The Awakening by Kate Chopin

There was no one to help Edna with her journey. Society was too strong to fight and no other characters were willing to sacrifice themselves for the journey. She was left alone and was faced with a choice between death or a return to her old life and her old self. She couldn't face isolation if she flaunted convention and did what she wanted with her life, and she couldn't face what society would do to her children because of her actions.

Gender-Bending: *American Beauty*

Lester found no support for his decision to change his life and to give up the notion that real men must perform, provide and protect. He wanted to find himself without returning to the safe dysfunctional world he came from.

CRAFT TIPS FOR STAGE 7 OF THE FEMININE JOURNEY

❂ Have you ever felt down and thought you were the only one in the world who felt that way? And then realized thousands of other people were going through the same thing? Use your own life history for ideas.

❂ Make sure you have planted your hero's helpers in the beginning of the story so they don't seem to appear out of nowhere. They should be people we heard about in Act I or passed by in Act II, so when they're recalled the reader remembers them.

❂ The hero will still face the villain, but she's faced all her demons and is stronger and more prepared for it.

Stage 8: Rebirth—The Moment of Truth

Sarah gathers all of her tools as she walks past the gates once more. She steps into the light and everything, though still the same, seems completely different to her now.

From a positive active stance she goes after her goal. She is no longer the fearful little girl who only knew how to react to the events in her life but a strong woman who makes things happens.

The hero has found her strength and resolve, and she goes after her goal with gusto. Nothing can stop her now. Tyrants and ogres would only find themselves laughed at in this stage. She sees the big picture of life and realizes she can't ever go back to the woman she once was and she doesn't want to.

She dusts herself off, grabs her new powers and walks straight into the lion's den. She isn't afraid to die because she realizes she was already dead in the perfect world. She tasted success during the eye of the storm, and it felt good. Now she wants it all. She can't believe she ever considered giving up during the descent.

The hero has learned to set boundaries, take action and listen to her own inner voice. She has reclaimed her identity and her weapons and realizes she is the creator of her own fear. She has found her courage, used her brains and won her own heart. The three combined are needed to attain her goal.

Having heart isn't to say the hero can't kill, if that's what the story calls for. Having heart means to have a consciousness, a sense of connectedness and responsibility for one's actions. It is to act from a place of calmness like the samurai instead of a place of reactive rage like a beast. With heart she has power. She's not reacting out of fear but acting out of power and truth.

Her goal is within reach. She must take the final step. "Will she do it?" is what the reader should be thinking. Sometimes this stage mirrors the stage of Descent when she first met the villain face-to-face.

She takes the final steps to show her transformation.

Where she once cried she now laughs. Where she was once hesitant she is now eager. Where she was shy and unsure she is now bold. Where she was tough and unfeeling she is now caring and considerate. Where she was once soft she is now a hard fighter. She now embodies the opposite of her former coping strategy.

Examples of Stage 8

The Descent of Inanna translated by Wolkstein and Kramer

When Inanna descends from the underworld two of Ereshkigal's demons follow her to find a replacement. Inanna won't let them take any of her children. When she comes upon her husband "Sitting upon a lofty throne . . . he used my powers to make himself more important . . . he refused to descend from his throne to help me." She challenges him to make the same descent she has and fixes the eye of death on him. The demons take him away.

The Wizard of Oz

When the Wicked Witch of the West tries to kill Dorothy and her friends, Dorothy picks up a bucket of water and splashes the Wicked Witch, killing her instead. She then demands the Wizard grant their wishes and she faces another illusion when she sees the Wizard is nothing more than a small old man without any real powers at all.

She learns she always had the power to return home within her. She just had to come to that realization. When she looks back at all she overcame on her journey she can see how strong she really was.

Titanic

Jack supports Rose throughout her descent and encourages her every step of the way. When things get tough he doesn't leave her. He guides her through the ordeal, telling her to hold her breath and wear a life jacket. He makes her promise that she'll survive no matter what and he sacrifices his life for her. When he dies, she lets go of his hand and is able to swim to safety and freedom. She's able to pull herself together.

On the Carpathia rescue ship she's given one last chance to turn back to the perfect world, especially now that Jack is gone. She hides herself from her fiancé and goes into the new world with a new identity.

The Awakening by Kate Chopin

Because Edna couldn't find support on her journey, her journey came to a tragic end in the last stage. Some say she chose to kill herself because that was the only way she could find freedom and that the ending is a happy one. She asserts that her life is hers to destroy and that she won't buy into the illusions that society puts in front of her.

Gender-Bending: *American Beauty*

Likewise, Lester couldn't find support and was killed in the previous stage. His death showed him the value of life, as the entire story is told in a flashback by the deceased Lester, who isn't bitter but has found peace.

CRAFT TIPS FOR STAGE 8 OF THE FEMININE JOURNEY

❂ Come up with five different ways to show her rebirth. Make sure they're all motivated. Look again at her fears.

❂ Think of all the symbols of birth and rebirth. Can you use an object that will symbolize her journey throughout the story and add it to the background setting to enhance the theme?

❂ Once this stage is figured out you may need to go back to Act I and filter in more elements of the theme of her journey.

❍ You'll need to add foreshadowing to the beginning of your story to cover up any holes that have come up to make this stage believable.

Stage 9: Full Circle—Return to the Perfect World

Sarah returns to the perfect world a fully realized person. She can clearly see the glass bubbles encasing her friends and desperately wants to help them all.

One friend stands up and hits her head on the glass ceiling. She looks up as if this is the first time she's ever bumped her head. With a smile Sarah walks toward her.

The hero returns home to see just how far she's come. She has attained her goal, but is she capable of facing this perfect world again without being pulled back into her old role?

This stage is a smaller climax where the hero returns to the perfect world and sees it for what it is. Through her experience others are changed and may even be forced to face their fears. She was once like them but now lives a better life. Does that mean it's possible for them to change as well?

Most often the person she was closest to prior to her awakening will be the one most influenced by her transformation.

She may pick someone to make the journey and continue the cycle, sharing her experience with others. She is the support for the next wave of journeyers.

Many women writers feel their stories are episodic, continuing like a circle rather than ending in a straight linear line. Some say the female story model doesn't have an ending at all.

Female stories do have endings, women do attain goals and they do make concrete changes in their lives and characters, but sometimes a hint of a life beyond the linear line, one that continues around into a circle, can be seen in this final stage of the journey.

Whereas the masculine hero "gets the girl" or an external reward in the end, the feminine hero gets something internal, a reward of spirit that continues on. Just because she has attained her goal and changed her life doesn't mean society has changed right along with her. There will still be tyrants, ogres, racists and sexists in the world; she's just more equipped to deal with those obstacles now.

Since the story itself has an ending that allows her to complete her journey or task, it leaves the reader with a sense of hope that women can accomplish and be successful. For those who want to write female stories without endings, another option is to consider using this stage to establish the circular narrative and allow the hero a successful resolution in the previous stage, even if success is abandoning her goal. Moral questions can still be asked here and not every subplot has to be tied up nicely.

Examples of Stage 9

The Descent of Inanna translated by Wolkstein and Kramer
Dumuzi's sister pleads with Inanna to help Dumuzi. She vows to take part of his time in the underworld, six months out of the year, and Inanna accepts her offer. His sister is a metaphor for the compassionate side of Inanna who will descend again to help others on their journeys.

The Wizard of Oz
In the book, Dorothy returns to the perfect world. She comes running toward her aunt. Clearly a lot of time has gone by and everyone knows she has been away somewhere, giving her journey validity. Her uncle built a new house, which is a symbol of all the changes she has been through. She can't wait to tell everyone what happened to her, and they can't wait to listen.

In the film, Dorothy tells everyone about her journey but they don't believe her story. She says she never should've left home, that she should only look for herself in her own backyard and not venture off. Once she returns to the perfect world she is under its spell again. "There's no place like home and I'll never leave you again," she says. No one even listens to her story or pays attention to her journey, and none of them will benefit from her experience.

Titanic

The beginning of the film starts with this stage as the older Rose shares her experience with the crew searching for the diamond. Everyone is captivated by her story and their view of history from scientific data is forever changed.

The film ends with her on the back of a boat, a similar place to the perfect world of the Titanic in the beginning. She holds the diamond necklace and drops it into the ocean, and we see pictures of all the things she's accomplished over the years—flying, horseback riding and going to the Santa Monica Pier. Her granddaughter cries as she listens to the story, changed by what she hears.

The Awakening by Kate Chopin

The return happens at the same time as the death stage. Edna returns to the Grand Isle, the place where the story started, to end her life. She pauses for a moment and watches a bird beating its wings as it falls into the ocean, recalling a tale she was told from the beginning of the story.

Gender-Bending: American Beauty

In a roundabout way, Lester returns to the perfect world through the telling of his story in first-person narrative after his death. He sees everything differently now and he wouldn't change anything.

CRAFT TIPS FOR STAGE 9 OF THE FEMININE JOURNEY

⊘ Look again at Stage 1 and mirror some of the elements in this stage to show how much she's changed. Does she react differently to the perfect world?

⊘ Can you change some of this world as a metaphor for her change?

⊘ Will she stay in this old world as a new person? Or will she walk out on the old world altogether?

⊘ Will someone be willing to listen to her story? Or will they be angry at her for changing?

⊘ Does she even want to return?

Chapter 25

Plotting the Masculine Journey

The masculine journey is a journey in which the hero gathers allies and tools to set out toward a goal. He rejects the feminine journey of inner exploration, faces death and either endures the transformation toward being reborn and is victorious, or he rebels against inner growth and finds failure. In victory his journey ends with questioning authority and his role in society and by finding his authentic self. In this new story model the hero is given a chance to awaken in Act III, but it's a chance he may not take. The nine-stage process is represented in three acts mirroring classic story structure.

The nine stages of the masculine journey are:

Act I: Challenge
1. The Perfect World
2. Friends and Enemies
3. The Call

Act II: Obstacles
4. Small Success
5. Invitations
6. Trials

Act III: Transformation
7. Death—A Fork in the Road

8. Awaken or Rebel
9. Victory or Failure

Act I
Stage 1: The Perfect World

A man named John stands looking up at Mount Everest. "I know I can climb this mountain," he thinks. "Many men like me have died here but I'll succeed. Everyone's counting on me."

John has spent years dreaming of climbing this mountain. He has the power, stamina and the whole of the world behind him, cheering. He takes out his equipment and climbs.

The whole world seems filled with opportunities. The hero has only to decide what he wants. Society tells him to succeed, to be a real man. He hasn't asked himself what success means to him yet, so he follows society's lead.

If the hero starts out asking, "What's this all for?" and takes steps to immediately change his life, as in *American Beauty*, then he's going on the feminine journey. If he's not willing to examine himself and face his inner demons, then he walks right past the stage of descent and focuses on his outward goal only. He'll get the girl, kill the bad guys and save the town instead of facing his symbolic death and transformation.

As discussed in chapter 23, there are three main societal expectations that may push men to succeed: performing, providing and protecting. These expectations unconsciously motivate the hero and serve to keep him from seeing and exploring other directions in his life. He gets tunnel vision as he pursues the ideal that's been laid out in front of him instead of pursuing what he truly wants for himself. Jed Diamond discusses this in his book *The Warrior's Journey Home: Healing Men, Healing the Planet*: "Not having a center to resonate from, we men take our cues from the outside. Our greatest fear is that if we lose or let go of external forms—the house, the spouse, the rules, the status—we will fall into a terrifying emptiness."

The three expectations:

⚙ **Performing:** A real man is concerned with career accomplishments or performs hard labor for a living. This man believes that career accomplishments equal success and manhood. "If I get that promotion, raise or partnership I will have made it," he thinks. "I just have to hang in there, network like a dog, and it will come." Becoming a team player goes hand in hand here and that further suppresses his true desires as an individual. Relaxing and just "being" aren't allowed; he must go go go no matter the cost to his family and health.

The hero can have a job in manual labor and also be seen as a hardworking successful man. The more hours he works the better.

⚙ **Providing:** A "real man" must make lots of money and be able to provide for his family whether his wife works or not. This hero believes that if he has money he's made it. How he gets that money isn't the issue, only that he has it. He's been told that it's OK for women to work or not to work, but he has no choice in the matter.

Sometimes the responsibility of being expected to provide for his family can drive a man to do crazy things. This isn't to say that women don't provide and face the same stress; society demands that men fall into this role. Men don't feel they have the option to stay home with the kids as a career, and if anyone should be providing it should be him.

⚙ **Protecting:** A "real man" protects the weak, seeks revenge and doesn't show his emotions. This hero lives by a tough guy code. He sees it as his job to protect the innocent and be the rock for everyone to lean on. Even the Woman's

Man archetype can fit here, thinking he has to protect women from bad marriages and open their eyes to the world. Does he ever get to see how his obsession to protect, be tough and emotionless deprives him from living a free life himself?

In most shoot-'em-up action, western and karate films we never get to really know the hero beyond his muscular exterior or dark stare. We never get to see the person he is or what he cares about, beyond revenge and duty.

The New Story Model
In the new story model for these heroes we see a change in Act III where the hero can veer off course and take a part of the feminine journey toward self-discovery and self-analysis and growth. The better action films have this stage.

In Act III of *Three Kings,* the three heroes find their emotions getting the better of them as they decide to give up the gold to save the people they've come to understand. They don't use guns and toughness to try and save the people in an impossible situation.

In Act III of *The Matrix,* Neo is reawakened by love (emotion and feeling) in the end—like Sleeping Beauty—and he wins not by using weapons but by believing in himself and "letting go." Essentially, Neo awakens in Act I and is on the feminine journey, but he also goes through a second awakening in Act III.

So while your hero may be set up as a typical tough guy, everything can change later on to allow for a strong character arc to take shape even though he isn't on the feminine journey of inner transformation.

✪

Stage I also shows his support system. He may:
✪ Seem to have everything.

✪ Have a lot of friends around him.

✪ Be told that he's the best, given awards, etc. Gilgamesh the King is called "Supreme over other kings, lordly in appearance . . . he walks out in front, the leader. . . ." Usually this type of opening sets the hero up for a big fall by the end of the story. His ego is so inflated he can't let go of the power it brings him and he suffers for it.

✪ Have a wonderful career ahead of him and a solid bank account.

✪ Be the most attractive man on the construction site. Arnold Schwarzenegger, Sly Stallone and Steven Seagal all have that tough muscle man charisma that elevates them above everyone else. As does Jackie Chan with his skills.

This stage also hints at the missing element in his life— nature, "the wild man lurking within," as author Robert Bly puts it. He isn't in touch with the greater whole, the connection and relatedness we all share together. He has suppressed his emotions, and he looks at the world as a scientist rather than a participant.

Many films about war show emotionless men fighting and killing who later stop and look around at all the destruction around them. The image of the soldier carrying a child to safety in the end of these films shows how much that character has changed since this stage.

He usually meets any one of the supporting character types who is in touch with the natural, instinctual, primal side of life, the part he's lacking.

Examples of Stage 1

Gilgamesh translated by Maureen Kovacs

"The first tablet opens with a narrator praising the wisdom of Gilgamesh, a famous king of old who left eternal monuments of both his royal and personal accomplishments." Life is grand for Gilgamesh. He is worshipped, respected and feared. His world is perfect except for his own longing to prove himself.

Star Wars
Luke Skywalker's life is OK. He's not happy with the way his uncle forces him to stay on the farm, but things aren't too bad for him either. He feels a responsibility to help provide for his family, but he wants to become a Jedi knight. He desperately wants "off this rock."

Three Kings
The Gulf war is over and all the men, who have been forced into the role of protectors for their country, are having a party because they get to go home soon. Archie (George Clooney) is having sex with a reporter. Everything seems to be going his way.

Moby Dick *by Herman Melville*
Ishmael travels to a small town in hopes of seeing the world and broadening his horizons. He finds a place to sleep and gets passage aboard a ship but there's a hint that his adventure will be less than perfect. The world is not as perfect as he'd like to imagine it to be.

Gender-Bending: *The Long Kiss Goodnight*
The film opens showing us a pleasant small town celebrating Christmas. Samantha/Charly (Geena Davis) is playing Mrs. Claus in the town parade. She has a party at her house with all her friends around her, and life seems perfect, except for the fact that she has amnesia.

CRAFT TIPS FOR STAGE I OF THE MASCULINE JOURNEY

✪ Remember to think about the pressure he feels to keep plugging along in life as he has been.

✪ This stage uses what he cares about to keep his blinders in place.

✪ Come up with five different ways to show his blinders.

✪ Remember you're introducing your hero to your reader in this stage and setting up the theme of the story.

✪ Just like in the feminine journey, it helps to think about what happened to the character just before the opening scene to add some color to it or reveal more about his character.

Stage 2: Friends and Enemies

John climbs the mountain. The air grows thinner and colder. His fingers freeze to his gloves. He feels the weight of his backpack on his shoulders. He's tempted to stop for the night, throwing him off schedule.

In the distance he sees the light of a campsite. Others are out here with him, and he takes comfort.

In this stage a friend or enemy comes on the scene, pushing the hero on and leading him to accept the forthcoming call. This character may:

✪ Have news the hero has been waiting for.

✪ Have information the hero has been trying to find.

✪ Save the hero's life.

✪ Be seen as competition for the hero.

✪ Help the hero meet someone else or network.

✪ Give the hero the tools he'll need later on.

✪ Give the hero an ego boost or confidence.

✪ Mess things up so badly for the hero that he's later pushed in a new direction.

Sometimes the hero needs the help of others to fulfill his

goal. How many people can rob a bank alone? Or drive a car and shoot at the same time? He may find himself alone in the end of the story, but for now he pulls together a team to set out on his journey.

This stage can be switched with Stage 3 depending on the type of story you're writing. If the hero needs help to find his calling then these characters come in to help him. If the hero has his goal and is answering the call to adventure, he'll later invite these characters in to assist him on his journey.

We really see the hero shine when he interacts with these characters. They can bring out his archetypal personality by either pushing his buttons so he reacts to them or by making him feel so comfortable he'll confide in them. Where would the loner cop be without the wise sidekick to drive him crazy?

Examples of Stage 2

Gilgamesh translated by Maureen Kovacs

Enkidu, the primal wild man, travels to Urk to fight Gilgamesh because of the horrible way he is treating his people. When Enkidu loses the battle he agrees that Gilgamesh's "strength is the mightiest in the land," and they become devoted friends.

Star Wars

Luke Skywalker meets C-3PO, R2-D2, Obi-Wan Kenobi, Han Solo and Chewbacca. Even though he saves the day alone in the end, he's now a part of a team that will support and teach him.

Three Kings

Archie learns someone has found the map to the gold. He tries to get it from them but realizes they can easily turn him in and then no one would get the gold. He knows he can't pull off stealing the gold all by himself, so everyone decides to team up.

Moby Dick

Ishmael meets Queequeg, and they both sign on as harpooners on the Pequod, Captain Ahab's ship. They make friends with the rest of the crew and become one of the guys.

Gender-Bending: *The Long Kiss Goodnight*

Many people surround Samantha/Charly. She has a daughter, a live-in boyfriend and a teaching job, but something is missing in her life. She can't remember who she is. She just woke up one day on the beach.

Investigator Mitch Henessey (Samuel L. Jackson) is the only one left who will work on her missing persons case for what she can afford. He becomes her partner as they try to find out who she used to be.

CRAFT TIPS FOR STAGE 2 OF THE MASCULINE JOURNEY

✪ Come up with five different ways to introduce the supporting characters here.

✪ Be creative with supporting characters. Change their age, sex and background until you find the best fit for the story. Make sure they're capable of contributing something to the story whether it's humor or expertise.

✪ You may hint at an inner problem in this stage. Use some of his archetypal flaws—greed, jealousy, etc., but this hero won't be ready to change or make the descent until the end of the story.

Stage 3: The Call

John makes it to the campsite and makes new friends, friends that seem to be on the same journey he is on. He feels at home with them.

The next day he wakes everyone up with the dawn and embarks on his climb once more, determined to reach the top first.

The hero either hears a call from someone else like a villain, or he hears the call of his own ego and sets out to attain his goal. He hasn't gotten in touch with his heart at this point and may not know what's really important to him or what it is he really wants.

Calls can come in several ways:

✪ **A Challenge:** The villain may be coming around to check him out, to see what the hero is made of. He'll throw the hero a bone and see if he bites. This draws the hero out into the open and may expose his strengths and weaknesses to the villain. The hero's desire to win and the drive to succeed fuels him; he can't resist the task at hand.

✪ **A Surprise:** The hero has been waiting for a chance to go after his goal but never expected the call to come; it seems to just land in his lap. Or, the villain is surprised because he didn't know the hero existed. This ups the stakes of the game for the villain, especially if the hero is unusually skilled or smart about things.

✪ **From Hero's Desire or Ego:** The hero creates his own call: "I need that . . ." or "I want this . . ." or "I'm the only one who can. . . ." He may be feeling the pressure to fulfill his duty and to help out, or he may be totally self-involved and want only to help himself.

✪ **A Red Herring:** The hero gets caught up in the wrong idea, path or goal. A supporting character messes things up for him and leads him astray, or the entire plot is based on a false belief another character puts into the hero's head. A lot of comedies start out this way.

✪ **An Order:** It's the hero's job to answer the call. He will lose his job and possibly his identity if he doesn't step up to the plate and accept the call.

Either way the hero is asked or pushed toward action at this point. Calls can serve several purposes:

✪ **Foreshadowing:** He achieves a small goal similar to that of the larger main goal of the story, like the man who runs in a marathon now and later runs to save a child.

✪ **To Wake Up the Hero:** The hero faces the first obstacle toward the main goal. He thinks things are easy and doesn't pay much attention to the goal or the villain until he faces the first tough obstacle. This is seen in action films where the hero comes up against the villain in the beginning, but much to the hero's dismay the villain manages to get away to fight again.

✪ **A Plot Twist:** The hero doesn't understand what's going on. He thought everything was all right, but the entire world seems to have abruptly changed around him. He's not sure who the good guys are anymore. Like Joe Turner (Robert Redford) in *Three Days of the Condor*, he goes out for coffee and returns to his office to find everyone dead.

In this stage what the hero cares about may be put in jeopardy by the villain or by the hero himself when he decides to go for the goal on his own.

Supporting characters may come out of the woodwork to laugh and ridicule him, telling him he's wrong, washed up and can't possibly accomplish what he's setting out to do.

Examples of Stage 3

Gilgamesh translated by Maureen Kovacs

Gilgamesh creates his own call. He is so praised by everyone that he feels invincible and at times bored. He decides that he and Enkidu will go to the cedar forest, cut down the sacred cedar tree, slay its guardian and become famous.

Star Wars
Luke Skywalker first receives a call in the message he finds from Princess Leia. He goes to see Obi-Wan Kenobi, who tells Luke, "You must learn the ways of the force if you're to come with me." Luke is still reluctant to leave his family, but when he returns home he finds his family and home destroyed by the Empire's forces.

Three Kings
The gold is the call for all the men in this film. The desire for money and the hope of securing their futures drives them. The call comes first and then the men team up together to achieve their goal.

Moby Dick by Herman Melville
Captain Ahab comes out of his quarters for the first time. He tells the men the story of Moby Dick and how he's driven to kill the whale. He says all the men on the ship are bound with him in his quest. He offers a gold piece to the first man who spots the white whale. All the men are enthusiastic.

Gender-Bending: *The Long Kiss Goodnight*
A group of carolers shows up at Samantha/Charly's house. When she answers the door a man with a gun steps out and tries to kill her and her family. She fights the man and manages to kill him. She has no idea where she learned how to kill as skillfully as she does. She has to find out why someone wants her dead, and she must leave to protect her family.

CRAFT TIPS FOR STAGE 3 OF THE MASCULINE JOURNEY

- ✪ What he cares about is put in jeopardy in this stage.
- ✪ The hero is pushed into action by his own desires or

by a villain.

✪ Remember to show the call instead of just telling it. What visual image can represent the goal at the end of the story? What will the hero need to learn to reach his goal in the end, and how can this be shown in this stage?

✪ Do any supporting characters laugh at him or try to stop him at this point? Or do they all support him?

Act II
Stage 4: Small Success

John is working his way up the mountain. The one man ahead of him falls, putting John in first place. Without wondering about the fallen friend John makes it to the top of the next peak hours before everyone else.

He sits happy in his accomplishment. He looks around and sees he has a lot farther to go to get to the top then he thought, but he's pumped now, invincible.

In this stage the hero has a small taste of success, which adds fuel to his desire to reach a much larger goal. He has answered the call and started on his journey. He met his first major obstacle and overcame it.

Pay attention to how this success affects the supporting characters around him. Are they happy for him? Jealous? Does this mean he'll be leaving them behind for a while as he sets out on a large challenge? Are they afraid for him? Do they try to make him feel guilty? Or do they ridicule him, trying to take the taste of victory from him?

He may have received warnings as he set out to complete this task, but he has ignored them and succeeded in spite of them. He feels he is invincible, that he is enough and doesn't need anyone else's help. His ego gets a boost, and he is pushed further from his center and further from self-awareness. Failure would push him to reexamine things; it would teach him humility.

If he lives more in tune with nature and is driven to protect others he may be very humble and down to earth on the one hand and very confident on the other as the heroes in *The Last of the Mohicans* are. They know they can overcome anything and are quick to take chances and risks for the things they hold dear.

Nathaniel (Daniel Day-Lewis) is successful in saving Cora Munro (Madeleine Stowe) and her sister Alice (Jodhi Max). He feels good about what he and his father and brother have done. He's secure in who he is and what he's capable of. Then he comes upon his friend's home and sees an entire family of women and children destroyed. He has failed them, and this both angers and humbles him.

Either way the hero wants more success:

✪ He knows he can do more.

✪ He doesn't want to sit back and examine things; he wants to go out there and do it.

✪ He wants to get that reward.

✪ He wants to succeed where others have failed.

✪ He wants to be "immortalized" for his actions.

He hasn't faced any major fears at this point. Most likely he has come up against a formidable task or opponent, but it's only a hint at what he'll have to face later on. Sometimes his success can be at a skill he learns, something he never thought he could do before this stage.

In comedies the hero may perceive the event as a success when everyone else around him doesn't think he was very successful at all. They think he's crazy but he sees only what he wants to see. It all depends on the hero's reference point. A guy who's down in the dumps, never able to get a date, may see one smile from a woman as "love." Lloyd Christmas (Jim Carrey) in *Dumb and Dumber* comes to mind.

Examples of Stage 4

Gilgamesh translated by Maureen Kovacs

Gilgamesh and Enkidu manage to slay the guardian, cut down the sacred cedar tree and achieve eternal fame. He is so pleased with himself he decides to go on a tougher mission.

Star Wars

Luke becomes very successful at his lessons. He is in awe of Obi-Wan as if he's the father Luke never had. With his help, Luke manages to rescue Princess Leia.

Three Kings

The men travel to a small village. They meet several of Sadam's soldiers who lead them straight to the gold. They fill their entire truck with gold bars.

Moby Dick by Herman Melville

After many days on the ship they meet several other ships at sea, the captain of each spinning tales of Moby Dick. Captain Ahab is overjoyed. He demands they tell him exactly where Moby Dick was last seen. He knows he's on the right track now and that nothing will stop him in his quest.

Gender-Bending: *The Long Kiss Goodnight*

They have a lead and agree to meet someone at a train station. They're ambushed, and Samantha/Charly is able to save herself and Mitch with her smarts and strength. She then learns that she was an assassin for the government.

CRAFT TIPS FOR STAGE 4 OF THE MASCULINE JOURNEY

✪ In this stage the hero gets a taste of success but hasn't really faced any of his fears yet.

✪ What assets would his archetype use? What fears would he fall back on?

✪ What do other characters think of his success? Are they jealous or supportive of him?

✪ Does he become more confident and cocky because of his success?

Stage 5: Invitations

John stands looking up at the mountain. His fingers are cold and sore again. He watches the last of the men make the ascent to where he stands. He starts to wonder why he chose to do this at all.

A man comes over; John's wife is on the phone. She wants to know why he's doing this. He can't answer her. He just knows he has to perform and he wants to succeed. Her questions only annoy him. He doesn't want to look at his emotions or question his choices. She reminds him of his dream to swim with the dolphins in the warm sun.

This stage is unique in that it may start with the hero being invited on a feminine journey. He is shown his flaws and asked if his current goal is his true goal. He is given an opportunity to drop his outward goal and go through an inner transformation.

In *The Last of the Mohicans*, Nathaniel accepts part of the feminine invitation when he places his love and emotions above his own safety. He stays behind as the other men leave the fort knowing he may be hanged for sedition. He can't leave Cora. He chooses to face death and the descent for love, for his relationship to another and not for his own gain. It isn't just about protecting her anymore but about how he's gotten in touch with his own emotions.

Most heroes walk away from such notions and continue on their path, but the invitation is always extended. The descent doesn't look too appealing to him. Facing himself and his emotions may be too much for him, even though he can physically and mentally do it all. He hasn't fully awakened yet. He won't let down his defenses.

❂ A character may ask him not to take part in the violence he's going to have to face.

❂ He may be asked what it is he really wants out of life.

❂ Friends may want him to give up.

❂ A lover may leave him because of his cold demeanor.

❂ He may be betrayed but chooses to ignore it as if it doesn't matter, or he seeks revenge.

This sets up the stage for his transformation or rebellion in the end. How set in his ways is he? How closed is his mind to changing? What will it take to open that mind?

Preparing for the Journey

Another part of this stage is the preparation for the journey. Now that he has chosen the outer journey he'll have many trials and obstacles to overcome. He'll meet them with resistance and with the hope of conquering them. He gathers the tools he thinks he'll need to accomplish this—guns, money, disguises, expertise. These tools mean survival and victory to him. Nothing will stop him now.

Armed with these weapons the hero feels confident, but he can't see what lies too far ahead of him; faith in his abilities keeps him going. Essentially it's his courage and willingness to grow that will make him successful, but he doesn't realize this yet.

A Mentor or Magi may show up with all the information

the hero needs, but the hero must find his own way of doing things. He's the only one putting his neck on the line, and he can't totally rely on the way of others.

In his mind he has a list of people he thinks he can call on if he needs assistance. There may be some characters he trusts. He may have a close friend he wants to share the journey with. What fun is it to succeed if there's no one there to see it?

On the other hand, he may be forced to work with other characters, which happens in many cop films where the lone cop wants to keep working alone but his boss forces him to take a partner.

Examples of Stage 5

Gilgamesh translated by Maureen Kovacs

Gilgamesh meets the goddess Innana after she has gone on her descent. She invites him to "marry" her to join with her— a metaphor for him taking the descent as she did. He refuses her, and the two become enemies. She sends the bull of heaven to kill him—after all, he went into nature, the territory of the Goddess, and slayed her trees. He refuses her and the descent to wholeness. He doesn't want to change his ways. Instead he gathers special weapons and sets out on his new journey.

Star Wars

Princess Leia shows Luke how strong and tough a woman can be as she helps them escape down a garbage shoot. When he first met her he seemed to be taken aback, as if he hadn't met many women on his planet. She is the "feminine" to him. She gives him strength and shows him the way as if she's been through it before.

Three Kings

Archie allows refugees to jump into the back of the truck. He was forced into a shooting match with Sadam's soldiers, and he can't just leave the people there to die now. He still doesn't care about the people as much as his pride. His life isn't in danger and the gold isn't in danger so he'll help the people to escape and show Sadam's soldiers who's the boss at the same time. He won't think too much about helping the people beyond that.

His truck is bombed, and a group of rebels help him and his men escape. They later ask Archie for help but he's unwilling to do any more.

Moby Dick by Herman Melville

Several times Captain Ahab is asked to give up his quest and examine his motives, but he won't take a look at what he's doing. He doesn't want to see himself as he really is. He doesn't want to face his rage; he just wants to blindly act it out.

Later, he meets with the ship *Rachel*. The captain begs Ahab to help him find his lost boat, which holds the captain's son. Ahab refuses, going against one of the codes of conduct and decency between captains. He refuses to help another.

Gender-Bending: *The Long Kiss Goodnight*

Charly won't face her old self (Samantha) now that she has regained her assassin identity. She changes her hair color and makeup and takes a shower. She's trying to wash the old identity away.

She tries to seduce Mitch, but he refuses because he knows she's only trying to bury Samantha the schoolteacher. He knows she wants to forget about her little girl back home. He wants her to face herself, but she isn't ready yet.

CRAFT TIPS FOR STAGE 5 OF THE MASCULINE JOURNEY

✪ Here the hero is invited down the feminine journey, but he refuses it. Come up with different ways to show his refusal. Is the woman in his life a metaphor for his feminine side? How does he treat her?

✪ This is the best stage to hint at whether he'll accept transformation in the end and grow or be rebellious.

✪ The villain can help push him on an outward goal to rescue what he cares about.

Stage 6: Trials

John continues to climb. The winds kick up. He can't breathe. The moon hides behind the clouds and darkness surrounds him. Another man has passed him and falls right in his path. John keeps moving forward, searching for a place to rest. He trips over the fallen man, hits his head and loses his water bottle.

In this stage the hero faces more obstacles to his goal. He may think he's overcoming all of them with ease and may expect it to be easy to defeat the villain, but he's wrong. No matter how successful he is in this stage it won't stop him from facing his worst fear in the next stage.

By facing his fears and overcoming obstacles, he's given another taste of success, which will fuel him and keep him reaching for his goal. If you want your hero to change in the next act, you need to gradually change his mind throughout this stage. Give him lots of reasons to change. Push him into that change.

Think of the hero in *Three Kings*. He doesn't just see poor women and children fighting for milk and change his whole outlook on life. He also sees soldiers stealing what little food they do have. He sees soldiers torture an innocent man, kill an innocent mother and harm a child. This is still only the beginning of his transformation.

Obstacles can be:

✪ Internal struggles and moral issues he has to face, like killing one to save the many, letting the villain get away to save someone, facing his own self-doubt or overcoming his own pride.

✪ External struggles that leave him exhausted—racing against time, physical ordeals.

✪ Mind games played on him by the villain. He may have to face his fears.

✪ A supporting character who comes in and messes things up for him.

✪ Red herrings thrown into the story to lead him down the wrong path.

✪ A villain who changes all the rules on him.

✪ A new villain.

✪ The thing he cares most about which is in jeopardy.

The strength and weaknesses of his archetype are tested here.

Awakening

If he's going down the path to awaken and change, this is when his defenses start to break down on him. He feels like his world is about to fall apart. He doesn't know who he is anymore.

If he's mental he is physically tested. If he can't face his emotions then he is thrust into an emotional situation. If he's greedy he is asked to sacrifice. Think of Ebenezer Scrooge in *A Christmas Carol*, who is so greedy and closed-minded he needs to witness the past, present and future of his life as well as others before he finally changes.

Also think of Martin Lawrence in *Bad Boys*. He has to

switch places with his partner. He goes crazy watching his partner spend more time with his wife then he ever did. He starts to feel bad for all the time he's lost with his family.

Think of Detective Sergeant Martin Riggs (Mel Gibson) in *Lethal Weapon* and how he fights to hold his emotions toward the loss of his wife at bay. He struggles to keep his defenses up.

Rebellion

If he's going down the path to rebel, then this is when he tries to beef up his failing defenses. He may become more rageful and unstable. Think of the character Rambo. Several characters try to reason with him and change his mind but no one can get through to him. He's on autopilot, fulfilling his mission like a good solider. He's like Captain Ahab in *Moby Dick*, blinded by his rage.

Even a good hero who rebels can get unstable taking risks he shouldn't take, doing whatever it takes to reach his goal. Think of all the karate films where the hero puts his life on the line because he's afraid to back down and lose face in front of people he doesn't really care about. Most of the time there is a master nearby who willingly walks away from the fight because he's secure with who he is. He's trying to teach this to his eager student who looks down on him for walking away.

Warnings and Prophecies

With rebellion usually come warnings against what the hero is doing or prophesies foreshadowing his impending doom.

In *Gilgamesh*, he has terrifying and ominous dreams. In *Moby Dick* Fedallah prophesizes several deaths.

Examples of Stage 6

Gilgamesh translated by Maureen Kovacs

When Gilgamesh refuses the feminine journey, Inanna sends the bull of heaven to fight him. He kills the bull, but since he has cut down the sacred cedar and killed its guardian as well, he has upset the gods. They decree that someone must die and that it must Enkidu. Gilgamesh is full of pride and will not be told what to do by Inanna. He insults her harshly because he is the king and can do anything he wants. He is his own worst enemy.

Star Wars

First they rescue Princess Leia from her cell, and the empire guards come after them. Then they find themselves stuck in a garbage disposal which turns on. They fight their way to their ship as Luke sees Obi-Wan fighting Darth Vader.

Three Kings

Archie realizes that his companion Troy (Mark Wahlberg) has been taken hostage. He needs the rebels to help him get Troy out. They make a deal—if Archie helps them get to the border they'll help him carry the gold and get Troy out of danger. Archie listens as the rebels tell their stories. He's moved somewhat by what they've endured and feels a little selfish for only caring about the gold. He doesn't know what good he can do but he now questions himself more. They leave and face many obstacles on the way to rescue Troy.

Moby Dick by Herman Melville

Captain Ahab must keep the crew in line. He struggles for control of the ship against those who might consider mutiny. He must guide the ship through the ice and deal with warnings

from other captains and Fedallah, a man on board who fore-
tells the future. Ahab won't change his mind, and he won't
listen to reason.

Gender-Bending: *The Long Kiss Goodnight*
Charly shoots several men in an alley who try to attack her, and
she learns that the government wants her dead. She decides to
get out of town, but she needs the money and passports she
has locked in a safe. However, her daughter has the key to the
safe so she'll have to go home to get it.

CRAFT TIPS FOR STAGE 6 OF THE MASCULINE JOURNEY

✪ Stretch your imagination about creating trials for him.
Does he have a hobby you can use?

- In *The Long Kiss Goodnight* Samantha/Charly knows how
  to ice skate, and there's a scene in the film where this
  skill is recalled. She puts on the ice skates, skates across
  the lake and is able to escape from the bad guys.

✪ Can a supporting character add conflict here?

✪ Make sure all his helpers, tools and expertise are
foreshadowed.

✪ His defenses will start to break down. Come up with
ways to show it, not tell it.

✪ Give him several reasons to change his ways if he'll
awaken. Try to persuade him to open his eyes.

Act III
Stage 7: Death—A Fork in the Road

John gropes around in the darkness and finds his water bottle. He feels for the
rope that will guide him back to camp as the fallen man moans behind him.

John wonders if he should risk his own life to help this man. He thinks it over for a moment and then drags the man back to camp with him.

Inside, by the light of the fire, John sees the man. It's a close friend of his, and he has died. He realizes if he hadn't fallen a few hours ago he could be his dead friend right now. Humbled and thankful, John thinks of his family back home, but he still wants to make it to the top.

At this stage the hero faces death and destruction. It's here that the hero is at a fork in the road. He can either face his own real or symbolic death and continue on the path toward awakening and victory, or he can rage against death and take the path toward rebellion and failure.

Awakening and Growth

Facing his own death means facing his own mortality, fears and shortcomings with grace and honor. He's humbled by the experience as he takes the feminine path of descent. It may make him lose sight of his goal temporarily, but he'll be forever changed by this experience.

✪ He may experience a "dark night of the soul" where everything seems completely lost to him and he acknowledges and accepts it.

✪ He may face the villain in a challenge that leads him to feel defeated and helpless, but he finds courage from deep within.

✪ He may face the death of a close friend or family member and see himself in their place.

✪ He may put his life on the line to save another as Nathaniel does in *The Last of The Mohicans* and as Jack does in *Titanic*.

His tools fail him; his strategy falls apart. He's left with nothing and may be at the villain's mercy. Can he temporarily face humiliation? He has to go with the flow of events and do his best. He has to stop resisting and stop trying to control and dominate the course of events. He's shown courage and now he needs to use his brains and find his heart.

Look over Stage 4, The Descent, in the feminine journey. Use the seven issues outlined to make him face an inner demon. In the feminine journey the hero goes on a slow descent and then faces turmoil in the death stage. In the masculine stage of Death, if he awakens, the hero goes through both feminine stages almost at the same time. It's down to the wire for him, and he's running out of time. If he's lucky, a supportive character will come and help him and push him in the right direction.

Rebellion and Stagnation

When he rages against death he's also raging against his own transformation. He's confronted with his own mortality and tries to become vengeful. If he faces death through the loss of a loved one, he wants to avenge that person and therefore prove himself superior to death. He won't die. He can't die. He won't acknowledge his fears.

He isn't at all humbled by his experience:

✪ In fact, he builds up his own ego to try to prove that he's more than a mere human being.

✪ He may take risks without thinking and will demand to fight the villain alone.

✪ He's like a one-man show of crazed masculinity who doesn't need anyone or anything.

✪ He won't face what the villain is showing him. He won't look inside himself to find out what he really wants out of life.

Supporting characters may push him to seek revenge, especially if he's idolized or looked up to. They keep him from making the right choice. If he's a leader or ruler he may feel pressure to keep it together and hold his emotions and feelings at bay. In *Braveheart* the one man who can help William Wallace is persuaded by his sickly father to betray him for the sake of his people.

Examples of Stage 7

Gilgamesh translated by Maureen Kovacs

"Endiku suffers a long and painful death, attended to the last by his beloved Gilgamesh, who watches by his deathbed and pours out a torrent of memories about their experiences . . . the fame he has achieved is nothing in the face of bodily decay. Gilgamesh rebels against mortality and sets out to find the secret of eternal life."

Star Wars

Luke has to watch helplessly as Obi-Wan stops fighting and accepts his own death. He screams out, causing the empire guards to come after them again. Once their ship makes it out of the death star, Luke is overcome with remorse for his friend. He is more upset now than he was when his aunt and uncle died, but he's able to pull himself together for the benefit of the mission.

Three Kings

Archie and the men face death as they fight to free Troy. He tells Conrad (Spike Jonze), "Do the thing you're scared of and get courage after you do it." They rescue more people as they rescue Troy. Conrad is killed, and Troy is badly wounded. Archie saves Troy with his medical kit and helps to prepare Conrad for burial. He wanted to be taken to a shrine so they decide not to bury him yet but carry his body with them.

Several rebels are killed and they perform the funeral rites.

They then bury the gold after giving each one of the local people a gold bar to start a new life. Archie has learned to care about these people and feels badly.

Moby Dick by Herman Melville
The ship is damaged by a severe storm, but Captain Ahab won't change course. Several men die, and the ship almost sinks. He thinks he sees Moby Dick swim by, but the men say he's hallucinating. Some think he's quite mad.

Gender-Bending: *The Long Kiss Goodnight*
Charly travels home and finds the key in her daughter's room. She looks outside and sees her daughter in the scope of her rifle and lets her guard down a little. She wonders if she's doing the right thing by killing Samantha, her alter ego. Her daughter is kidnapped, and Charly makes the decision to save her life.

Both Charly and her daughter are captured and face death together in a locked freezer.

CRAFT TIPS FOR STAGE 7 OF THE MASCULINE JOURNEY

✪ Read Stage 4 of the feminine journey and use the seven issues of descent against the hero if he's on the path to awaken.

✪ Once this stage is figured out, you may need to go back to Act I and filter in more elements of the theme of his journey.

✪ Use his assets to help him to victory or his flaws to bring him failure.

✪ Externalize his feelings. Think about his reactions to events around him.

✪ Use his fears against him.

Stage 8: Awaken or Rebel

John knows in his heart that he wants to continue to the top of the mountain. He also wants to honor his fallen friend by taking his friend's scarf with him. He ties it around his arm and continues on his journey upward, a little less cocky than before.

He tells the others what happened when he reaches them, and they agree to stay together to make sure they all make it.

If the hero ends the last stage able to face death, he moves toward awakening in this stage. If the hero chooses to rage against death, he moves toward rebellion in this stage.

Awakening and Growth

The hero learns from his experience. He faces his flaws and his fears. He looks back on all he's done and realizes what his true purpose in life is. He's no longer a slave to what society says he must do, but the active creator of what he truly wants for himself. If he hasn't been active enough this is where he truly acts and says "no" to what he doesn't want, just as the feminine hero does in Act I of her journey. He sees beyond the illusion of what everyone else is telling him he should do, and he figures out he has some soul-searching to do. He's no longer in a revenge mode.

The hero may:

❂ Remember what he wanted to do for a living as a boy.

❂ Reflect on how much time he's lost with his family.

❂ Ask forgiveness for the wrongs he has done in the past or on his journey. Stories of redemption fall here.

❂ Decide to leave a relationship or job that's abusive to him.

❂ Come to terms with his flaws and failures.

❂ See his greater connection to the whole and no longer fear death.

✪ Decide that he hasn't been doing all he can to reach his goal and put forth more effort. He may have been afraid to stand up to his boss.

Rebellion and Stagnation

In this choice the hero becomes more like a villain. The hero doesn't learn from his experience. He doesn't face his flaws or admit his fears. And he certainly doesn't look back on all he's done to realize his true purpose in life. He's blinded by his fear of death and failure. His goal may change to include some way for him to prove his superiority over life and death itself. He wants the elixir that will resurrect him from death's grasp, and he'll give up his original goal to get it.

The hero usually remains the same throughout the story even though he reaches the goal in the end. He doesn't examine himself, his beliefs or his motivation.

He may:

✪ Get more guns and fire power.

✪ Push everyone else aside as he moves forward alone.

✪ Forget about everyone and everything that ever meant anything to him to reach his new goal now.

✪ Go out of his way to hurt those who try to stop him.

✪ Justify his actions in any way necessary to keep his consciousness at bay. This is easy for him if a loved one has been sacrificed by the villain.

Whichever path the hero chose in the last stage, he now takes steps down that path. The rest of the journey seems mapped out in front of him. His decision has declared his fate.

Examples of Stage 8

Gilgamesh translated by Maureen Kovacs

Gilgamesh is warned of his impossible quest as he searches for the man who can bring him immortality. He meets this man and fails at the immortality test to go without sleep; he has no faith in himself. He is sent home with a plant that will allow him to relive his life with his current knowledge, but he doubts this and winds up losing the plant. He returns home empty-handed.

Star Wars

Luke decides to fly in the mission to bomb the death star. He's confident in his ability to fly as he did "back home," but when it comes time for him to take the final shot at the death star he must let go of what he's learned in the past and awaken to the power that lies within him instead of without. He tells R2-D2 to "increase the power!" but it's the words of Obi-Wan that put him on the right track—"Let go, Luke, use the force, trust me." The success from his previous lessons helps him to believe in himself.

Three Kings

Archie's real awakening comes when he decides to give up the gold and abandon his own goal and welfare for the goal and welfare of others. They've gotten the rebels to the border and they know they're breaking the law and will probably be sent to military prison. They call a reporter to the scene to help get the rebels' message out to the public.

Military helicopters show up, and they hold hands with the people. They try to run them across the border before the helicopters can land, but they don't make it. Archie looks around at his men, and they all nod in agreement—use the location of the gold to bargain for the freedom of all these people.

Moby Dick by Herman Melville

Captain Ahab has rebelled. He goes after the white whale. For three days they fight the whale but are unable to kill him. Men die all around him, but Ahab won't give up. The prophecies come true, but still he won't relent. His rage has taken over. He stabs at the whale and is dragged to his death.

Gender-Bending: *The Long Kiss Goodnight*

Charly not only has awakened to her power as a spy but she now awakens to her power as a mother. She takes care of her daughter and talks to her about getting a puppy as she devises a plan of escape.

They make it out but she has to rescue her daughter again. She lays on a bridge dying as she tells her daughter to run for it, but her daughter won't go. Charly, for the first time ever, calls on a CB radio for help. She realizes she's not alone and that she has a responsibility to help others. She isn't a one-man wrecking crew who can do whatever she likes and risk death every moment of the day. She learns to care about others and therefore herself.

CRAFT TIPS FOR STAGE 8 OF THE MASCULINE JOURNEY

❂ If the hero awakens, show his inner turmoil and changes.

• In *The Matrix*, when Neo turns around and faces the deadly agent instead of running, his whole demeanor shows us his inner transformation. He waves his hand like Bruce Lee, calling the agent out, reflecting back to the training scene when he fought Morpheus.

❂ Can a supporting character try to persuade him against this decision?

✪ Come up with different reactions for the villain to have toward his decision. Will he raise the stakes even higher?

Stage 9: Victory or Failure

All of the men make it to the top together. John is ecstatic. He forgets how important it was to him to be the first and only man on the top of the mountain. It doesn't matter anymore.

He turns around and relishes the view—his reward. He looks across the horizon and down at the climb he endured.

Victory

If the hero chose to awaken in the last stage he now finds victory and reward. Because he knows who he is and why he's striving for his goal he has the courage and know-how to face anything the villain may throw at him.

If he's fighting to save more than just himself he has the whole of the group behind him. He makes sacrifices and appeases anyone he has to in order to reach the goal. He isn't concerned or ruled by his ego any longer and will admit defeat to win, meaning he would humble himself at the feet of the king in order to save the entire kingdom.

Failure

If the hero chose to rebel in the last stage, he now finds failure. He won't give up his ego or sacrifice himself for the greater good. How he looks to others is most important. He'd rather be the king with control of the kingdom than the one humbled at his feet to save the kingdom.

His rebellion has led him down a path of no return. His blindness has kept him from the truth about what's important to him, and it also kept him from facing and overcoming his fears. He hasn't grown much from where he started out.

He may realize he has failed by the end of this stage and find redemption, like the samurai who commits suicide to keep his honor. He looks back and sees his mistakes now but realizes it's too late to change things. Think of Captain Ahab in *Moby Dick* or Willie Loman in *Death of a Salesman* by Arthur Miller.

He may still be stuck in rage and denial until his last dying breath, accusing others of bringing about his demise. A lot of historical stories about kings and kingdoms fall into this category.

Be careful not to fall into the B movie trap. Low budget films abound with tough guy heroes who run along a plotline, killing and fighting without a shred of remorse, who get the girl and all the glory in the end. These stories take a hero who has chosen failure and give him rewards. Imagine if Captain Ahab had killed the white whale in the end and survived— what would that say about his obsessive behavior? How satisfying would it be? How would it change the story? Would it still be a masterpiece?

Examples of Stage 9

Gilgamesh translated by Maureen Kovacs

Gilgamesh returns home empty-handed and has to face his friends and family. He thinks about all the decisions he has made in his journey, but he also realizes it's too late to change his mistakes.

Star Wars

Luke lets go and trusts himself and the force around him. The death star is obliterated. He, Han Solo, Chewbacca and the droids receive medals from Princess Leia and admiration from her people.

Three Kings
Archie and the men make it home. The reporter aired such a great piece on the plight of the rebels that the military couldn't put them in jail. They all find careers and get on with their lives knowing they did the right thing.

Moby Dick by Herman Melville
Captain Ahab meets a watery grave. Moby Dick the white whale wrecks all the boats, kills those who would have killed him and swims away without a scratch on him.

Gender-Bending: *The Long Kiss Goodnight*
Charly saves her daughter, herself and all the people who would have been killed by the villains. She has the money from her safe at her side as she tells the President of the United States that she'll go back to her life as a schoolteacher. In the last scene we see her hair a mix between Samantha and Charly's style. She throws a knife into a tree and smiles as her boyfriend sits next to her.

CRAFT TIPS FOR STAGE 9 OF THE MASCULINE JOURNEY

 ○ **Victory**—is he proud of his decision? Does he see himself as victorious, even if he's changed goals as a result? Does he have to face a boss who'll be angry with him like the heroes in *Three Kings* do?

 ○ **Failure**—how badly will he fail? Does he hold himself responsible or does he blame others?

 ○ **How do other characters react?**—Do they walk away from him if he's a failure? Do they criticize the victor who may have changed goals?

Appendix

U se the following worksheets to outline your story. Jot down how your character might act in each stage.

THE FEMININE JOURNEY WORKSHEET

Act I
Stage 1—The Illusion of a Perfect World
- She has a false sense of security and is trapped in a negative world that stops her growth.
- She avoids the reality of her situation by using a coping strategy.
- Your character: _____
  _____
  _____
  _____

Stage 2—The Betrayal or Realization
- Everything important to her is taken away, and she can't ignore or make excuses for what happened.
- She's pushed to a fork in the road where she must make a decision.
- Your character: _____
  _____
  _____

Stage 3—The Awakening—Preparing for the Journey
- What will she do now? Her coping strategy is of no use to her any more.
- She actively prepares for her journey and makes a life-changing decision to move forward.
- She wants to reclaim her "power."

- Your character: _____

_____

_____

Act II

Stage 4—The Descent—Passing the Gates of Judgment

- She faces one of her fears or obstacles and may want to turn back but can't.
- Her weapons won't work; they're useless here.
- She faces some of the Seven Issues. (See pages 220–221.)
- Your character: _____

_____

_____

Stage 5—The Eye of the Storm

- She comes to terms with the ordeal she just faced and thinks her journey is over.
- She has a false sense of security.
- Supporting characters may want her to come back.
- Your character: _____

_____

_____

Stage 6—Death—All Is Lost

- Total reversal happens.
- She faces her own death or a symbolic one and learns more about herself.
- Your character: _____

_____

_____

Act III

Stage 7—Support

- She accepts her connection to the group. She's part of a larger whole.
- Hopefully someone or something supports her now or she may not make it. Support gives her a way out of the darkness.
- Your character: _____

_____

_____

_____

Stage 8—Rebirth—The Moment of Truth

- She has found her strength, and she goes for her goal with gusto.
- She has awakened and sees the whole world differently.
- She has come into her power in a healthy way.
- She faces her worst fear and still remains compassionate and complete.
- Your character: _____

_____

_____

_____

Stage 9—Full Circle—Return to the Perfect World

- She returns to see how far she's come.
- She may pick the next person to go on the descent.
- Your character: _____

_____

_____

_____

THE MASCULINE JOURNEY WORKSHEET

Act I

Stage 1—The Perfect World

- The world seems full of opportunities for him.
- He doesn't know what he truly wants deep down inside.
- Your character: _____

  _____

  _____

Stage 2—Friends and Enemies

- Friends help push him toward a challenge.
- He may find helpers and assistants.
- Your character: _____

  _____

  _____

Stage 3—The Call

- Unsure of what he wants deep down inside, he goes for an outward goal.
- Possibly what he cares about is put into jeopardy.
- Your character: _____

  _____

  _____

Act II

Stage 4—Small Success

- Small taste of success gives him the desire to reach higher.
- How are others affected by this success?
- Your character: _____

  _____

  _____

Stage 5—Invitations

- He's invited down the feminine path to awaken.
- He's asked if his current goal is what he truly wants.
- He says "no" to the feminine path and gathers his weapons together. He won't give up any of his power.
- Your character: _____

  _____

  _____

  _____

Stage 6—Trials

- He faces obstacles.
- If he's on the path of rebellion he has a false sense of superiority.
- If he's on the path of awakening things seem to be falling apart for him.
- Warnings and prophecies may surround him.
- Your character: _____

  _____

  _____

  _____

ACT III

Stage 7—Death—A Fork in the Road

- Rebellion—he rages against death and fights his own transformation and change.
- Awakening—he faces death and is humbled; all his tools are useless. (see feminine Stage 4.)
- Your character: _____

  _____

  _____

  _____

Stage 8—Awaken or Rebel

- Rebellion—he won't face his flaws or face change. He has no character arc because nothing has changed for him.
- Awakening—he faces himself and knows what he truly wants. He gives up some of his perceived power in order to be successful. He's willing to help others.
- Your character: _____
_____
_____
_____

Stage 9—Victory or Failure

- Rebellion—brings him failure. He's down the path of no return.
- Awakening—brings him victory and rewards.
- Your character: _____
_____
_____
_____

JOURNEY DIFFERENCES

Feminine Journey	Masculine Journey
Ending provides a circular or episodic framework.	Follows a linear line with clear beginning, middle and end.
She proves herself to herself.	He proves himself to the group.
It's multi-climactic.	There's one major climax.
She returns to share her experiences with anyone who'll listen and chooses the next one to partake the journey.	He returns to share his rewards with the entire group. He's taken the journey for them.
She travels the path of allowance with obstacles.	He travels the path of resistance to obstacles.
She awakens in the beginning when she realizes she never had power. She comes into "self" to be awakened.	He awakens in the end when he realizes his power holds him back from his feelings. He must let go of "self" to be awakened.
In her model she finds "heart."	In his new model he finds "heart."
She finds courage.	He finds courage.

SOCIETAL/GENDER DIFFERENCES

Feminine Journey	Masculine Journey
She's kept from her journey if saved.	He's told to save and protect women.
She's told to be passive and receptive.	He's told to provide and be strong.
She gets internal reward of "spirit" and selfhood.	He gets the girl and external rewards in the end.
She learns about nature and oneness.	He learns about courage and oneness.
She needs to trust herself and her own instincts.	He needs to trust his abilities.
She lives in a dangerous world.	He lives in a world of opportunity.
She isn't supported by society.	He is supported by society.

INDEX